REPRINTS OF ECONOMIC CLASSICS

INSTITUTIONAL REVENUE

INSTITUTIONAL REVENUE

A STUDY
OF THE INFLUENCE OF SOCIAL INSTITUTIONS
ON THE DISTRIBUTION OF WEALTH

by

H. D. DICKINSON

M.A.(Cantab.)
Lecturer in the Department of Economics
University of Leeds

REPRINTS OF ECONOMIC CLASSICS

AUGUSTUS M. KELLEY · PUBLISHERS
NEW YORK · 1966

FIRST PUBLISHED 1932

LIBRARY OF CONGRESS CATALOGUE CARD NUMBER

66-21368

PRINTED IN THE UNITED STATES OF AMERICA
by SENTRY PRESS, NEW YORK, N. Y. 10019

CONTENTS

PREFACE

This book was conceived and planned during a course of study undertaken at the London School of Economics and Political Science during the years 1922–24 and rendered possible by a research-studentship awarded by the School. An outline of the main argument appeared under the title 'Institutional Revenue' in *Economica* (No. 11, p. 186—June 1924). I acknowledge my gratitude to Dr. Edwin Cannan, my supervisor in studies, for continuous guidance and pains-taking criticism. Dr. Hugh Dalton gave me valuable criticism and advice. To my friend, Maurice Dobb, I am particularly indebted. In the course of numerous discussions he and I worked out in common many fundamental notions, although we have developed them along individual lines—he in his *Capitalist Enterprise and Social Progress* and I in the present work. Thus many of the ideas to be found in the following pages owe much to his inspiration.

Since I left the London School of Economics in 1924 the work has been subject to many interruptions and suspensions. A portion of it was abandoned; the remainder has been enlarged and revised in many directions and has taken a form very different to that of the original plan. For encouragement during this period I am indebted to my friend and colleague, the late J. R. Taylor.

H. D. DICKINSON

THE UNIVERSITY, LEEDS
January 1, 1932

INSTITUTIONAL REVENUE

CHAPTER I

INTRODUCTORY

1. No social fact is more obvious than that of inequality in
the distribution of wealth. No other economic circumstance
has a greater influence upon human welfare. Although
the average magnitude of the social income is important,
yet changes in it do not produce such an effect on the
body politic as changes in the manner of its distribution.
A man in estimating his material welfare looks more to
his position as compared with his neighbours than to the
absolute amount of material wealth at his disposal. Thus
a community may grow richer without being aware of it;
it may even grow poorer without being conscious of much
privation, if all its members participate similarly in the
change: but let there occur an alteration in the shares
enjoyed by different individuals, classes, industries and
localities, then, even if the average level of wealth is
unchanged, immediate attention is directed to the phenomenon.

2. The plain man may take up three different attitudes
towards the causes of inequality of wealth. In the first
place he may consider them as chance variations and
take them for granted in the same way as he takes the
unequal portions of good looks, health, physical strength,
and intelligence that fall to the lot of mankind. He either
does not attribute them to anything at all or else attributes them to such unverifiable causes as luck or the
will of God. In the second place he may attribute them

to inequalities in personal economic value, due to the varying amounts of intelligence, skill, industry, thrift, and business acumen exhibited by different men in the conduct of their affairs. According to this view some people get more than other people because they earn more or are worth more than other people. In the third place, he may ascribe inequalities in wealth to force or fraud exercised by those who enjoy a share greater than the average. Whereas both the first and the second views in their different ways attribute economic inequality to 'natural' inequality and regard it in some way as inevitable, this last outlook attributes it to artificial and arbitrary interference with the order of nature and regards it, usually, as modifiable by other, often violent, interference.

On reflection, none of these theories are found to be adequate. Leaving aside the pure luck theory as being the negation of any scientific sociology, we find elements of truth in the other two. The second, or personal efficiency theory affords a fairly satisfactory explanation of economic inequality between individuals who have enjoyed approximately equal opportunities, but it fails to account for the great difference in the conditions of classes in a class-stratified community. A man may rise, by virtue of his superiority to his fellows in industry and ability, to the ownership of a large business, but his son, even though he is not distinguished above the common, may succeed him and continue to enjoy an income above the average: indeed, the son may give orders to and control the lives of men who are his superiors in those qualities by which his father rose in the world. Although it might not be far wrong to assume that, of two professional men or of two labourers, the one that made the bigger income was the more able and the more industrious, it would be rash to assume that every successful professional man is more able and more industrious than any labourer. This is obvious in societies where class distinctions rest frankly on legally maintained inequalities and privileges. For instance, most people would agree that the personal efficiency of the serf as compared with the lord had practically nothing to do with the difference in their economic condition. But even in societies in which equality before the law is fully guaranteed and in which all are free to compete in the struggle for wealth and power it is clear that other forces besides personal efficiency decide the award of the prizes.

The third, or grab-what-you-can theory is equally unsatisfactory. Although some income in all communities is acquired through undetected (or unpunished) stealing and cheating, no society can continue to exist that allows complete licence to its members to take what they will how they will. Apart from the devastating effect upon social cohesion and morale that such a course of action would have, there would soon be brought about a state of things in which there was nothing for anyone to take. Even a band of robbers has agreed rules for the division of the spoil among themselves. Moreover, a robber band can only go on robbing so long as there are law-abiding merchants and farmers producing wealth for it to levy toll upon. Income-getting by force and fraud is essentially exceptional: it implies a background of orderly economic activity and a normal process of income-getting that does not involve force and fraud. But here it may be objected that the economic order itself is nothing but legalised robbery and extortion, and that certain normal processes of income-getting are only socially sanctioned forms of force and fraud. Legalised robbery is, of course, a contradiction in terms: the phrase as usually used implies that the person using it considers ethically wrong certain forms of economic activity permitted by society as a whole. But the phrase does involve the idea that the socially sanctioned forms of getting an income have something to do with the relative magnitudes of different persons' incomes: it diverts our attention to the social institutions under which income is acquired.

3. If the plain man, tired of theorising on his own, asks the professional economist what causes the inequalities of wealth, the answer that the latter gives will vary according to the school of his upbringing or of his predilection. If he belongs to one of the offshoots of the Historical School he will reply by a dissertation on inequality in the past, on Enclosures and Mercantilism, on Usury Laws and Serfdom. If the economist belongs to the Analytical School that is orthodox in Great Britain he will probably offer in reply to one question the answer to another. Instead of giving an explanation of why some people are rich and some poor, he will divide income into various categories of wages, rent, interest and so forth, and explain how each of these species of income arises and what determines its magnitude. These manœuvres often succeed in making the plain man think that his question has been answered, but sometimes they leave him feeling that he has been made the victim of some kind of confidence trick. Nevertheless, the academic economist of either school is so far right inasmuch as the plain man's question cannot be adequately answered until social institutions have been discussed and until the problem of distribution between categories such as wages and interest has been solved. The analytic economist's mistake lies not in analysing and explaining the genesis of the different income-species, but in not pursuing the matter further and analysing the social institutions under which the accepted laws of return to factors of production give the results they do. The mistake of the Historical School lies in imagining that a descriptive treatment of social insti-

tutions alone can give an insight into the effect of institutions on the distribution of wealth.

4. In discussing the influence of social institutions on the distribution of wealth, we are considering simultaneously two subjects that are too often kept separate and treated as belonging to two distinct branches of study. The distribution of wealth is part of the general body of economic theory: it is usually discussed as a special application of the all-prevailing theory of value and hardly thought of as involving human beings in their social relations at all. The comparative study of institutions, although of approximately the same age as the study of economics, has far fewer systematic theories and attractive generalisations to offer the student. It is often approached from the side of jurisprudence, of political science or of moral philosophy; less often from the side of economics. There are, nevertheless, two ways in which economics and the study of institutions can give mutual service.

One is the working out of theories that interpret social forms and social development in terms of economic causation, the other is the endeavour to show how the apparently abstract and universal propositions of economic theory presuppose certain social institutions and are relevant only to them. In the first direction much has been done towards the construction of a coherent body of theory, the so-called materialist conception of history. Unfortunately, in the hands of most of its exponents it assumes too doctrinaire a form and it is forced to supply explanations of historical events that are more ingenious than plausible. As a methodological instrument it is of great value, but as a complete sociological synthesis it is, even at its best, premature. The economic analysis on which most of its upholders base it is definitely fallacious. Nor does it take sufficiently into account the social implications of recent advances in psychology and anthropology.

The second way in which economics and the study of institutions have blended has developed out of the efforts of the Historical School of economists. Starting as the chroniclers of different forms of economic life and of their transformations and developments, the writers of this school gradually emancipated themselves from the abstract attitude of the classical economists and their successors and began to formulate economic theory in terms of changing forms of social organisation. Unfortunately their theoretical concepts tend to lose precision and completeness almost in proportion as they show a real historical sense of the relativity of economic theory to social development.

No attempt will be made here along the first of these directions. An economic interpretation of history if it could be based on an accurate and complete economic theory and a systematic and thorough-going comparative study of institutions, would be worth constructing, not because it is necessarily the only valid interpretation of history, but because any unitary conception of history is a useful frame of reference in which to organise knowledge. The economic theories presented here may contribute an integral part to such a generalisation, although they are an insufficient basis for it in themselves. Perhaps some day a complete theory of social institutions will be developed that will explain their evolution and transformation, and will even attain the scientific precision of analytical economics, in that it will make possible predictions as to the probable results of making this or that change in the fundamental groundwork of social life. But such an achievement is not yet. In any case it is not the present writer's purpose to formulate such a theory.

The object of the present book is to approach the

problem from the second of these two directions. Certain
social institutions of economic importance will be studied
from the point of view of economic theory. Current
economic theory will be criticised in the light thrown
by economic history on the validity of its assumptions,
but its abstract and deductive method, instead of being
superseded in favour of a historical and inductive one,
will be retained and amplified by taking into account the
facts of social institutions in their varied forms.

The method of the orthodox political economy of to-day
is to proceed from the theorems of pure economics, by
the successive introduction of modifications and exten-
sions due to the working of actual institutions, to the
conclusions proper to an existing form of society. However, a sufficiently clear distinction is not usually drawn
between pure economics and the economics of a particular
society. On the one hand, propositions in pure economics
are held to be valid for forms of society where the working
of certain institutions may modify their action: on the
other hand, propositions relevant only to particular social
systems are often taken as valid for all economics.

5. Since the middle of last century the study of economics
   has proceeded along two paths which have rather diverged
   with the passage of time than tended towards a common
   meeting point.

   The publication of *The Principles of Political Economy*
   by J. S. Mill in 1848 marked a resting-stage in English
   economic thought. About the same time a similar stage
   of development was reached on the Continent. The
   analysis of the classical school had been extended and
   completed into a neatly rounded-off system; everywhere
   the economist sat back in his chair, surveyed his handi-
   work, and saw that it was good. Mill believed that he
   had said the last word on the subject of value: it was

generally considered that 'cost of production', 'supply and demand' and 'free competition' provided an adequate answer to every question that could be asked of economic science.

Four influences combined to rouse economists from a disastrous complacency.

The first was the German historical school. Starting with Roscher, followed by Hildebrand and Knies, there arose a school of writers who had a method of thought and a set of assumptions quite different from those of the classical school. They tended to be inductive rather than deductive, concrete rather than abstract; they preferred the detailed investigation of phenomena to general principles and abstract categories, like value, rent or competition. They extended the field from which they drew their inductions far wider than the classicists, who concentrated their attention almost exclusively on contemporary conditions in commercially well developed Western countries. Furthermore, the historical economists had a wider intellectual background in history, philosophy and comparative law. Thus they did not fall so much into the classicists' mistake of assuming that the particular social and economic framework of nineteenth century Europe was 'natural', a form from which any other social economic order was a deviation. Hence it was easier for them to recognise the dependence on social institutions of the distribution of the social product. Meanwhile, the economists of the Historical School and of its offshoots, the sociological school of Wagner and Max Weber and the neo-socialist school of Oppenheimer, Sombart tended in their reaction from the abstract treatment of the analytic school, to neglect economic theory altogether. The typical writers of this school showed the defects of their qualities; in their hands the science, in becoming history, ceased to be economics. They abandoned the search for general principles altogether and ignored analysis.

Thus economics became divided into two distinct sciences: analytical economics and economic history. The principal contributions to economic theory, at any rate in English-speaking lands, have come from followers of the first specialised study. The founders of the historical school, however, have had a slowly permeating influence on the pure economics of the past sixty years: a tendency to conceive the body economic as an organism rather than as a machine, as a thing capable of dynamic developments as well as of static equilibria; a growing recognition of the social point of view in economics side by side with the individual: a gradual abandonment of the naïve assumption of the fixity and universality of existing social institutions. Their influence is to be traced in the Austrian School, at first sight so extremely abstract and 'pure'. It is just this wider sociological outlook that makes the work of Menger, Böhm-Bawerk and Wieser a more fundamental and permanently valuable contribution to economic science than those of Jevons and Walras.

The second influence was that of the higher mathematics. The mathematical school had two forerunners, Cournot and Gossen, but their work was ignored until Walras and Jevons founded the school and popularised in their respective countries the ideas of final or marginal utility.

The third influence was Carl Menger, a great and original thinker who seems to stand alone, owing little to prevalent streams of thought, yet starting many new ones. He was the founder of what is most characteristic in modern economics—the analysis of demand at its origin in the mind of the economic agent—and founded the psychological or Austrian school. He introduced the concept of marginal utility (evolved independently by

the mathematical writers from a rather different standpoint) while his followers elaborated the general idea of
margins. In this country, in spite of the efforts of Smart,
Wicksteed and a few others in more recent years (especially Henderson), the influence of Menger was never fully
felt. It was strained through the eclectic meshes of
Marshall, who weakened some of its best points in the
attempt to keep it within the categories that J. S. Mill
had stereotyped in British economics.

The fourth influence was the socialists and the reaction
against them. On the Continent, Marxism, the economic
theory of which was professedly based on that of the
classical economists, had become the dominant socialist
school. Surplus-value became the focus of attention and
the effort of orthodox economists to put the theory of
interest on an unassailable foundation was one very strong
influence on the development of economic theory. Here
must be mentioned the works of Böhm-Bawerk, Irving
Fisher and Gustav Cassel, the first two of whom were
true disciples of Menger.

Here also come the American writers who developed
the Productivity theory. While Böhm-Bawerk and Fisher
admitted that interest was a surplus and gave an explanation for it, J. B. Clark reverted to the old idea of cost
(under a new form) and controverted, with considerable
ethical force and much complacent satisfaction with
existing institutions, the idea that interest or profits could
be in any sense an 'unearned' element in income. Much
as we owe Clark for introducing into economic analysis
the distinction between the static and the dynamic, we
are forced to admit that his theory of static economy
represents a mental throw-back to the days before John
Stuart Mill.

The last three of the four influences mentioned above
worked all in the same direction. They revivified the

moribund body of classical economics and developed out of it the modern analytical school. Writers of this school immensely enriched the analytical power and subtlety of economic science, but unfortunately they turned economics from the study of the dynamic elements in society to that of the static elements as they work under existing social institutions.

In Great Britain and America, where new ideas are accepted reluctantly, unless they can be shown to be really old ideas in a new form, the first shock of the new analytical tendencies in economics was absorbed by Alfred Marshall, who by skilfully grafting the ideas of the Austrians and of the mathematicians on the old classical stock produced the still green and flourishing tree of the English orthodox economic school. Since then the most important tendency in analytical economics has been a tendency to eliminate the psychological substructure of the Austrian theory (while retaining the concrete superstructure of marginal equilibrium) and to return in spirit though not in substance to the objective methods of Smith and Ricardo. The chief exponents of this neoclassical tendency are Cannan and Cassel.

6. The present work is an attempt to combine the analytical method of the modern marginal school with the historical economists' recognition of the existence and influence of social institutions. It contains the outline of a theory of distribution which, starting like the modern orthodox theory with the theory of value based on the concepts of marginal utility and substitution, will exhibit more clearly than that theory does the influence of certain social institutions.

It is the author's intention to show that the strictest adherence to a theory of marginal valuation is perfectly compatible with a view of distribution that takes fully into account the part played by the social framework. For this reason he has gone into greater detail than might at first seem necessary on the subject of value. He has recapitulated the marginal theory of value in order to show that it fits logically into a complete system that takes in both institutions and utility. A second reason for such a restatement is the fact that even to-day writers of the marginal school are far from having reached complete agreement on many points. In view of this uncertainty the author has preferred to state his own views in full rather than to indicate them by reference to the works of others. The theory of value to which he gives his adherence is the marginal-utility theory of the Austrian school, as expounded by Menger, Wieser and Böhm-Bawerk: he has also been considerably influenced by the 'objective' price theory and the interest theory of Cassel. He attempts, however, to go beyond the individualistic and atomistic outlook of the Austrian School and of its neo-classical successors and tries to consider the 'return to factors of production' as determined by the social framework within which the process of valuation operates. There is developed the concept of a new category of income, Institutional Revenue, which is capable of playing a rôle in social and historical analysis similar to that of the Marxians' surplus value.

7. It is now possible to outline the plan of the present book. First will be given a brief review of social institutions with definitions and explanations. No profound treatment of institutions will be attempted—only enough to lay the foundation of the subsequent theories. Since the theory of distribution between factors of production is really a branch of the theory of value, a discussion of the theory of value must precede that of distribution. The theory of distribution then falls into two divisions: distribution between factors of production, and distribution between individuals and classes. After the different factors of production have been enumerated and defined, their mode of co-operation described, and the forces that determine their respective returns have been made clear, a basis has been obtained on which to found an investigation into the measure in which the factors are supplied by individuals; how far one person supplies many factors and how far his contribution is limited to one; how far persons supplying a particular factor form classes with distinct economic opportunities and interests; what circumstances control the opportunities of individuals and classes for supplying factors of production; and how these circumstances affect the return to the factors and hence the distribution of income among persons of the community.

Thus the main argument of the present work will be divided into four parts:—

1. Discussion of Social Institutions;
2. Theory of Value; leading up to
3. Theory of Factor-distribution;
4. Theory of Personal Distribution.

CHAPTER II

DISCUSSION OF SOCIAL INSTITUTIONS

1. It is almost impossible to define a social institution satisfactorily. Individually, a social institution can be recognised and described, but it is difficult to frame a definition to which it will not give the lie in the course of its development. To frame a definition of social institutions in general is a still harder task.

   The word 'institution' is used in two different senses: sometimes it denotes a way of life or a set pattern of social behaviour with regard to some function or functions; at other times it denotes the organisations in which this way of life is embodied or which preserve and maintain it.

2. Taking the first sense first we note that the idea of function is inherent in the idea of an institution. We may define a function as a type of specific human activity. Every institution is based upon a function or upon several functions. It is not only a way of life, but a way of life with respect to some function or functions. The way of life is a general and an involuntary one: all persons living in a community partake of its institutions. Not only can no purely individual type of behaviour be counted as an institution, but no type of behaviour that, though it involve common activities, any individual is free to follow or not as he choose. Thus Parliamentary Government is an institution, but not the Labour Party; Religion is an institution in most stages of civilisation, but it ceases to be when freedom of thought has unravelled the close interweaving of religion with education and with civil obligation and has made it a matter of personal choice to which of 'the two-and-seventy jarring sects' a man will attach himself.

3. Coming to the second sense in which the word institution is used, we note that it denotes an organisation or association of human beings with certain objects (not necessarily conscious) connected with the pattern of social behaviour just referred to. Sometimes they organise in order to prosecute the activities in question: we can then say that the organisation embodies the pattern of behaviour. Thus corresponding to Government we get the State, and to Religion we get the Church. Sometimes we get an organisation of men for the purpose of defending or maintaining some way of life, some general framework of activity. For example, the State may give positive sanction for some particular system of Economic Freedom (maintenance of Property and Contract) or of Unfreedom (regulated Gilds or Castes). Or again, within a particular institutional framework certain permanent and regular forms of organisation may spring up for the purpose of furthering some particular interest of men, such as the Joint Stock Company under Economic Freedom; the Trade-union, the Gild, the University, Parliament, in connection with various other institutions.

Not all institutions have an organised embodiment of this sort. For instance, Economic Freedom expresses itself in a number of individual acts, but they take place within a general framework of custom, convention and positive law that justifies us in calling Economic Freedom a social institution. Again, the institution of Marriage is embodied in a number of married couples, in rights and duties associated with their married status and with the complex of social observances that concern them, but married persons are not organised into associations of the married.

In any of these three ways or in others, the difference between the two meanings of the word Institution is one of abstract and concrete. In this book we shall reserve the term Institution for the first or abstract sense, and use the words organisation or association to denote what is often called an institution[1] in the second or concrete sense.

We can thus define an Institution as a set pattern of social behaviour with respect to some function or functions. We can further remark that some Institutions are and some are not embodied in definite organisations or associations.

4. In order to deal with the diverse institutions that have existed in human society at different points of space and time some classification must be attempted. The word 'function' should be the keynote of any really scientific classification or description of institutions. If the object of the present work were a complete natural history of social institutions, its foundation would be an analysis of human behaviour and a classification of the forms of man's normal activity. Each of these forms of activity would be what we have called a function and each function would be the nucleus of an institution or set of institutions. Here, however, social institutions will merely be grouped under a few provisional heads, each distinguished by some title of general import.

An empirical classification of institutions is into:—

1. Economic Organisation

Economic Organisation in the narrower sense {
(a) Labour Organisation
(b) Organisation of Enterprise
(c) Political Organisation

2. Property (including Inheritance and Contract)
3. Status
    (a) Class
    (b) Order
    (c) Caste

[1] Cf. R. M. Maciver, *Community*, Bk. II, ch. iv; *The Modern State*, p. 6. Also G. D. H. Cole, *Social Theory*, pp. 41-43.

4. The Family (including Marriage)
5. Education
6. Religion

This classification is admittedly imperfect. Much is omitted; what is included is badly classified. For instance, the separation of Property and Contract from Political Organisation on the one hand and from Organisation of Enterprise on the other, is a purely artificial one, due to the special importance of Property and its allied institutions and to the fact that in the past it has received separate treatment. Status and the various forms of Organisation overlap and interlock. Nor does the order in which Institutions are enumerated here correspond to the historical order of development. The order adopted in this book is determined partly by the relative importance of institutions at the present day and partly on grounds of logical convenience in introducing and defining new concepts.

5. It would be a mistake to treat all these institutions as so many separate and unconnected entities. Our rough classification must not induce an atomistic way of regarding institutions. Having analysed them we must then effect a synthesis. This synthesis is the concept of a social system. All functions, both of individual and of social life, are interconnected and interdependent. Hence, both in their development and in their functioning, the institutions that these functions underlie must form a correlated whole. For instance, certain forms of Marriage imply certain forms of Property and of Economic Organisation. Not only is Property closely connected with Economic Organisation, so that different forms of one can only exist with certain forms of the other, but certain forms of Political Organisation are correlated to both. This whole, this complex of all social institutions serving all the functions of man, is called a Social System.

6. 1. ECONOMIC ORGANISATION

Economic activity is essentially social. In fact we may define economic organisation as social co-operation for economic ends. The purely self-regarding economic actions of the individual are so few as to be almost negligible; although for the purposes of analysis or illustration we may consider such individual acts, they are unreal abstractions until they are combined into a whole of social significance.

Every time we use 'our own' money to purchase goods or services; every time we sell, save, work for wages or fees, we enter into an economic relation that is the first link in a chain of economic relations that involves every human being in the civilised world. The buyer and the seller may think that their transaction affects only themselves; a little reflection should show them that it affects all those to whom the buyer may sell and from whom the seller may have bought, the number of whom increase with remoteness like the number of a man's ancestors. But this is not all: the original pair of agents affect all those to whom the seller might have sold or from whom the buyer might have bought if either had preferred to conclude his bargain with other competitors: thence the chain is carried backwards and forwards through a still greater number of collaterals. In some cases this is obvious. For instance, public opinion recognises that the terms of a wage-contract involve the interests, not merely of the worker and of the employer who engage themselves, but, through the competition of the labour market, the profits of all employers and the conditions of life of all workers in the trade concerned and, ultimately, those of employers and workers in all trades.

From this point of view the only purely self-regarding economic activities are those that could take place in a Robinson Crusoe economy: the production for one's own use of goods that one would otherwise go without and the disposal among various forms of ultimate consumption of resources already in one's possession in circumstances where their disposal will have no effect on subsequent acquisition of resources. It is usually supposed that Consumption falls under this head of self-regarding activities, and on this ground it is often omitted altogether from the science of economics; but, since as a rule the disposal of resources affects subsequent social economic action, Consumption can no more be exempted from the above somewhat sweeping dictum than Production and Exchange. The social nature of every economic action is a fact that tends to escape notice at the present day. Since economic life has become highly individualised, the individual is freer and takes action on his own responsibility more than under previous systems, but it still remains true that economic activity is social co-operation, though voluntary, and takes place in an institutional framework that determines its mode of working and its result.

All economic activities are, then, forms of social activity. They are examples of the principle of the social division of labour. In the course of them men create certain forms of organisation, embodied in certain types of association. Those forms of organisation that are essentially concerned with 'the social economy of an economic society',[1] as distinct from those, like the Family and the Church, that are not essentially (but may be incidentally) economic in function, we shall consider here under the head of Economic Organisation. From the propriety of including such forms of economic organisation as joint-stock companies, cartels, co-operative societies, trade unions and craft gilds no one will dissent. (Economic Organisation in the narrower sense, divided into Organisation of Labour and Organisation of Enterprise.) Objections may, however, be

[1] Oppenheimer, *Grundriss der theoretischen Ökonomik*, §1.

raised to the classification of Political Organisation under the same head. If the Church is to be excluded, why should the State be included? The reasons why we have dealt in this way with Political Organisation are that it is concerned as to nine-tenths of its activities with economic life (the State is in fact one of the most important mechanisms for regulating economic activity, even during the dominance of *laisser-faire*), and that in many periods of historical development its forms overlap and merge with those that are undoubtedly economic in the narrow sense (in medieval times the Borough and the Merchant Gild; in modern times the State and the monopolistic industrial Concern).

7. (*a*) *Labour Organisation.*—The institutions under which the labourer works are very various. The chief forms of organisation of labour are four: to wit (i) independent labour; (ii) wage-labour; (iii) serfdom; (iv) slavery; in the first two of which the labourer's place in the social system is defined by contract, in the second two by status. We may thus term the first two forms free labour, the second two unfree or bond labour. Independent labour is the condition of the personally free workman owning his own means of production, organising his own work and marketing his own products.[1] He is sometimes called the 'self-employed' labourer. Wage-labour occurs where the labourer is politically free and is free to change his employment and his trade, but where the means of production are owned by persons (entrepreneurs) other than those who work them. Serf-labour occurs where the worker, though he may own his own land and tools has no voluntary

[1] The last qualification is inserted because a specialised class of persons buying the labourer's product and marketing it may develop into a privileged class and exploit the labourer. In some cases the industrial capitalist evolved out of such a middleman. The American farmer to-day complains of this disadvantage.

mobility. Slave-labour exists wherever ownership of the means of production, personal freedom, and voluntary mobility are all absent.[1] Under all these forms of organisation various forms of association occur among workers. Thus independent labourers may own the means of production either individually or in groups; they may market their products individually or collectively. All kinds of workers (even slaves) may form benefit-societies, which often develop into societies for their own protection and ultimately for bettering their economic position. Thus these associations may serve four different functions: (i) organising or doing work itself (such as producers' co-operative societies, the modern 'guilds' and artels); (ii) regulating and controlling the conditions of work (such as medieval gilds, soviets, corporazioni and Betriebsräte); (iii) insurance and benefit (such as friendly societies and the Roman collegia); (iv) protecting the interests of the labourer in the sale of his products or services or in the wage contract (such as modern trade-unions, but associations belonging to classes (ii) and (iii) also serve this end). Of these four functions, the first belongs strictly to Organisation of Enterprise, the third to ordinary business undertaking; thus there remain the second and fourth functions. These may also be severally performed by other kinds of bodies not associations of workers, such as trade-boards. These bodies are usually in some way representative of the workers affected or of some of them. If they are completely non-representative, they must be imposed on the workers from above, either

[1] From the point of view of the master the 'mobility' of the slave is greater than that of the serf; for he can sell the slave to another master, while the serf is typically bound to the soil, and not to its owner, and so is immovable. But I am not referring to this kind of mobility, but to the mobility of the worker in the sense of a legal right to change his domicile and to enter into economic relations with whom he pleases.

by their employers or by the state. In such a case it would be better to classify them under Organisation of Enterprise or under Political Organisation. Thus we might define the function of Labour Organisation in the narrow sense as the autonomous or partly autonomous control effected over the conditions of labour by association of labourers or by bodies representative of them. This function appears to arise as a corollary of division of labour and collective production. It is embodied in associations such as societates, gilds, trade-unions or trade-boards.

8. (b) *Organisation of Enterprise.*—Enterprise involves the union of Business Organisation with the direction of the use of Capital. The provision of the latter involves the Organisation of Capital.

9. By Business Organisation is meant the initiation of production, the decision as to how much shall be produced, and what means of production employed, the control of the division of labour, the balancing of costs and the substitution of alternative means at the margin, on which all advanced economy depends. In modern capitalist society it is chiefly performed by a specialised undertaker, a business man, but it is still partly carried out, as it is wholly in pre-capitalist societies, by ultimate consumers or by self-employed workmen. Under pre-capitalist conditions there is little scope for initiative and enterprise: most production is regulated by custom and traditional right.

10. By Organisation of Capital is meant the institution or complex of institutions whereby is provided the accumulation of produced means of production necessary to society for the carrying on of its economic life. Two things are necessary for capital to come into existence: the saving, 'waiting', or postponement of consumption which sets

productive forces to be used for making intermediate (production) goods rather than final (consumption) goods; and the organisation that directs these productive forces into the right channels so as to produce intermediate goods in the right form, place and quantities. The first of these two things is an individual act, the second is a social function. It is the second that is referred to here.

11. The organisation of capital is so closely allied to business organisation that they are best discussed together. It seems natural that control over economic processes should go with the provision of the means whereby they are carried out; thus in nearly all social systems the two functions are provided by the same organisation or by closely related organisations. These two functions may be provided by different persons (as the managing and the sleeping partner) but they are nearly always combined into one organisation (the partnership). At the loosest, there is a closer connection between these two functions than between either of them and Labour. The combination of capital with business organisation may be termed Enterprise.

12. The different ways in which Enterprise is organised may be classified as follows:—

    1. Private Enterprise.

      (*a*) Individual Private Enterprise.

      (*b*) Associative Private Enterprise:—

        α. by associations of capital-owners (Joint Stock Companies);

        β. by associations of workers (Workers' co-operative societies, some Agricultural co-operative societies, the 'Guilds' of recent times);

        γ. by associations of consumers (the retail and wholesale co-operative societies).

2. Public Enterprise (essentially associative: sometimes called Collective Enterprise).

    (*a*) Managed directly by a State, province, county or municipality.

    (*b*) Managed by a Public Corporation, Commission or Trust.

Interesting developments are occurring in the direction of a blend of Private Associative Enterprise and of Public Enterprise. Such are the Port of London Authority and the Central Electricity Board set up under the Act of 1926 for the British electricity supply. Such also are the "gemischte Betriebe" of Germany and other continental countries: enterprises organised as joint-stock companies whose shares are held partly by municipalities or the State and partly by commercial companies. Projected organisations on these lines, but involving the principle of workers' control, were the scheme for the British coal industry outlined in the report of the Sankey Commission and the Glenn-Plumb Plan for the United States railroads.

13. Corresponding to these forms occur various forms of property in the means of production, private and public, individual and collective (see p. 36). This correspondence is not, however, a rigid one. For instance, public ownership may go with private organisation of enterprise, as in the case of a State-owned railway or telephone system leased to a commercial company for operation.

14. Important among the specific instances of the organisation of enterprise are the bodies that regulate the flow of liquid resources of a community. These are, in modern times, the banks and acceptance houses and the bill-brokers. The State in its capacities of tax collector and of large spender —sometimes also of large-scale conductor of enterprise—is

also important in this connection. Collectively they form the financial system. Essentially this system would appear to be concerned solely with the function of capital organisation, but in practise it has acquired at least two other important functions. In accordance with the natural tendency above alluded to, control has become associated with capitalisation, so that in many countries the control of industry has so concentrated as to result in the organisation of all large-scale production in comparatively few groups of closely allied interests, each group ultimately dominated by one or by a very few financial houses. The second function that the financial system has acquired is the virtual control of the emission and circulation of means of payment, in other words the creation of money, and the regulation of the price-level—a function the exercise of which has far-reaching consequences.

15. (c) *Political Organisation.*—Under Political Organisation, or Government, is understood the inclusive and compulsory organisation of the community as a whole, having as its object the preservation of the institutions of property, status, etc., on which the prevailing social order rests and having as its necessary consequence certain methods of acquiring revenue to cover the cost of its own functioning.

The function of Political Organisation is that of general organisation and administration: it is concerned not with particular economic activities but with the conditions under which economic activity in general goes on and with the regulation of the relations between the persons and organisations that carry on economic activity in particular. Political Organisation is distinguished from other kinds of Economic Organisation in that it embraces all the members of a community and not just some of them, and in that it wields the community's ultimate resources

of moral and physical force. This function is exercised
under modern conditions by the State, and under other
conditions by different forms of organisation, resting
ultimately on force. The State is characterised by its
definiteness of organisation and by the inclusion in it not
only of all members of the community but, at any rate in
theory, of all members in all their relations. It is a single
organisation claiming sovereign power over all its members
in all their relations. In this it differs from the political
organisation of societies in which there has evolved no one
single all-embracing sovereign authority wielding a monopoly of coercive power. Here would be the proper place to
discuss, were there time, the structure and working of the
modern State; the division into Legislative, Executive and
Judicial functions; the development of the Economic
State and the Administrative State out of the Legal State
and the Police State; and kindred subjects.

Thus the function of the existing State is the maintenance of the institutions of property, contract, and freedom
upon which capitalist production rests: it provides the
necessary funds from the revenue of public domains and
public enterprises, from taxation, from loans, or from the
profits of inflation. Under Political Organisation are not
meant all the economic activities of the State. There are
excluded many economic functions often assumed by it,
such as the provision of goods and services like an ordinary
entrepreneur, or the regulation and protection of labour
through Trade-Boards and Factory Inspectors. These are
its accidental, not its essential functions, and are to be
classified under the Organisation of Enterprise (b) or
under Labour Organisation (a) rather than under the head
of Government.

Inasmuch as the chief institutions of the social system
have a legal basis, the institution of Government provides
their ultimate sanction. Property and Contract are secured

by the coercive organisation of society; so, either directly through legally enforceable privileges or indirectly through property and contract, are all the different shades of status (class, caste, and order); so, paradoxical as it may appear, is economic freedom, since it is constantly liable to infringement and must as constantly be vindicated by the arm of the law.

16. 2. PROPERTY.

Blackstone in his *Commentaries on the Laws of England*[1] defines property as 'that sole and despotic dominion which one man claims and exercises over the external things of the world in total exclusion of the rights of any other individual in the universe'. R. T. Ely,[2] more cautious than Blackstone, defines it as 'the exclusive right to control an economic good'. He then proceeds to define similarly private property and public property as the right of a private person and that of a public body, respectively, to control an economic good. Ely thus restricts property to economic goods. Property-rights in non-economic goods, even if they could exist for the jurist, would be meaningless to the economist. The idea of exclusiveness occurs in both definitions.[3] Property must of course be construed relatively. From the point of view of any rational sociology absolute property-rights, like any other kind of absolute rights, are nonsense. Ely, seeking for the theoretical basis and justification of the institution of property, is driven to that of general welfare as the sole possible. Three things, therefore, limit the legal rights of any subject: the law of the land (no one can do, even with his own property, that which the law prohibits), the public interest (called, in the case of property, the 'eminent domain' of the Crown

[1] Bk. II, ch. i.   [2] *Property and Contract*, p. 101.
[3] For the definition of economic goods and non-economic goods, see p. 65.

or the State), and the similar rights of other subjects, guaranteed and secured by due process of law. The principle underlying all these is that of social utility. Property, like all other institutions, forms part of a social order, and the rights guaranteed under it can only be tolerated by society in so far as they contribute to the efficiency and safety of that order.

The institution of property takes very different forms, not only at different times and in different communities but at the same time and in the same community. Following Ely we may classify property-rights

    (I) according to the owning subject
    (II) according to the owned subject
        (A) in intensiveness of property rights
        (B) in extensiveness of property rights.

17. (I) Property can be either (1) Private, (2) Public. Private property can be either (a) Individual, or (b) Associative.

Public Property is essentially associative property: it may be called Collective Property. An intermediate stage between (1) and (2) is exemplified by the property of a quasi-public corporation. A quasi-public corporation is one, like a railway or water company, that belongs to a corporation of shareholders but in whose functions the public has so great an interest as to preclude the possibility of the proprietors' doing just what they like with their own. They may own it privately, but they must manage it as if it were public property. There are other intermediate stages; for instance a partnership is intermediate between (a) and (b). It is necessary to note the difference between public ownership and associative private ownership. In the latter case each member of the group has a definite individual interest in the joint property and may usually sell or otherwise dispose of this interest. A member of a political body that owns public property on the other hand frequently has no definite individual rights over it or over any part of it, may be excluded by his fellow-citizens from any share in the control of it, and cannot usually alienate his rights in any way nor even obtain compensation for their loss on emigration or secession from the body.

A form of public property that is, so to speak, only inchoate property is common property. Among most primitive peoples land is common property, as is the sea to-day among civilised peoples. Many remains of common property persist even in advanced communities, but they tend to be converted, either into public (collective) property, by the vesting of the rights in a particular political body; or into private property, by the mutual consent of the individuals enjoying rights in it to the division of the rights (or of their capitalised value) individually among them. Here there may be definite individual rights, even more than in the more usual cases of public property (e.g. compare a commoner with rights of estover or turbary with the ordinary citizen's interest in a naval dockyard). In other cases of common property, however, the rights are inalienable, and there is no definite and organised corporation in which they are ultimately vested. Consequently there is usually no guarantee of them nor redress if they are invaded, save in the unorganised force of public opinion.

18. (II) (A) Intensiveness has reference to the nature of the thing owned. One possible classification is—

1. Material Objects;
2. Personal Services;
3. Relations to persons and things.

Under this head come monopolies, patents, rights acquired under charters and public concessions, goodwill, contract-rights, civil rights.

Another classification, and one more significant for our purpose is—

(1) Consumption Goods.
    (*a*) durable;
    (*b*) non-durable.

(2) Production Goods.
    1. Labour
        (i) The Person of the Labourer. (This only becomes the object of property-rights under the Institution of Slavery.)
        (ii) The Services of the Labourer (Labour-Power, including contract-rights in personal services and some forms of goodwill).
    2. Capital Goods.
        (*a*) durable (fixed capital);
        (*b*) non-durable (circulating capital).
    3. Land (including mineral rights, fishing rights, etc.).

19. (II) (B) Property rights are more or less extensive according as the control exercised over the economic good is more or less extended. The sole and despotic dominion may be abridged in various ways:—

(1) By the separation of various uses of a thing and the vesting in different owners of rights in each use, as when the rights in a house are divided between the ground landlord, the builder-landlord and the tenant. The rights of different classes of shareholders and of debenture-holders in a company afford an example of a different sort of division of property rights.

(2) By the separation of various kinds of use of a good and by the regulation by separate arrangements of rights in each kind of use. For example the right of using a thing may be limited by the obligation to restore it in full

working order to some other person who, to the exclusion of the first person, has the right of using it and of wearing it out (*jus utendi et abutendi*). The right of destruction may be altogether reserved by a public body, usually in the public interest. In some countries a man may not set his own house on fire, in others the owner of a forest may only cut trees down under certain conditions, or the proprietor of a watercourse may not let the water run to waste. The right of use need not necessarily include that of alienation. Some goods may be incapable of being bought and sold (such as a slave, under some codes), others only under certain special conditions (such as Land, under the English common law).

(3) By the imposition by public authority of conditions under which the rights of use, etc., may be exercised. Not only the ordinary implicit restrictions of the law, that property may not be used to do any unlawful action or in contravention of other persons' legal rights, but more general restrictions, made in the public interest, may limit the rights of property. Under this heading may come not only the prohibition of destruction or waste, mentioned under (2), but also the general conditions under which, nowadays, a common carrier or other public utility operates. A railway is under a legal obligation to keep its equipment and rolling stock in repair and to run a minimum number of trains a day at a minimum speed, over every part of its line. If it obtains authorisation to make new constructions, it must complete them within a given time, or forfeit its authorisation.

(4) The exercise of property-rights may be limited in time, as in the case of patents and copyrights, and of terminable annuities. On the other hand, it may be extended beyond the lifetime of the property-owner so as to form the institution of Inheritance.

20. *Inheritance.*—The right to dispose of one's property after one's death is closely allied to the right of using it during one's life: it is subject to similar limitations. The institution of Inheritance is later in development than that of Property in general. To present-day Englishmen the right of settling the disposition of one's property after death appears as natural as that of disposing of it during one's lifetime. This was not always so and it is possible that all rights of private property were originally limited to the lifetime of the owner. Among less advanced peoples many cases occur where no freedom of bequest is permitted at all: the goods of the deceased revert either to the community or to the family or some to one and some to the other, movables sometimes even being destroyed entirely. Freedom of bequest appears to have been obtained first for movables, land and immovables still passing beyond the individual's control at death. Complete freedom of bequest is characteristic of a highly individualistic social organisation.

Even in our modern Occidental civilisation, most legal codes other than the English common law restrict the power of bequest in favour of the testator's family, reserving certain proportions of his fortune, in Scots law called the *legitim*, to certain relatives and dependants. The residuary rights of the community also are recognised, as in the middle ages by heriot and escheat and in modern times by legacy and succession duties, which are usually considered as different in nature from ordinary taxation. Both ancient heriot and modern death-duty may be considered as commutation-payments, wherewith the individual buys from the state or its representative the right to bequeath his property. The more restricted nature of Inheritance rights, compared with other property-rights, is recognised in the law of mortmain and similar legislation and in the power assumed by the state of setting aside bequests to superstitious uses, of changing the use and destination of charitable bequests and of modifying deeds of trust.

21. The functions of the institution of inheritance appear to be threefold: (1) the preservation of the system of private property; (2) the giving of a motive to the individual for accumulation of wealth beyond a provision for his own life; (3) the well-being of the family. To these Ely adds a fourth: the well-being of the whole community. But what is this but a general expression covering the first two? Presumably the institutions would not develop or would not long survive if the institutions of private property and of the family were not thought to be of social utility. Beyond these, what other utility has the institution of Inheritance?

22. *Contract.*—Ely defines contracts as 'agreements of economic significance which are enforceable by public authority'. They must be possible, legal, and not against public policy.[1]

We have already included rights obtained under contract among economic goods in which property-rights inhere. Ely and most other writers on the subject treat contract as different from property, while admitting their close relationship. Here it is included as a particular form of property. Whatever may be the justification in law for the distinction, there is none in economics. Rights obtained under either are of the same nature, are interchangeable, and have similar social effects. For instance, some income derived from land and capital is secured to its enjoyer by means of property-rights; the rest of income derived from land and capital and all that derived from labour and enterprise by means of contract-rights. Thus contractual rights can be classified according to the same

[1] *Property and Contract*, p. 562.

scheme as proprietary rights (pp. 36–39), according to the subjects and the object of the contract and according to the intensiveness and the extensiveness of the rights involved.

Again, the limits between contract and other forms of property are very narrow, in that the acquisition of rights in a thing may be tantamount to possession of the thing. Thus contractual rights to the performance of stipulated services by a person may come very near to actual ownership of that person. This is specially liable to occur when the persons in whom the rights are vested and the persons over whose services the rights extend belong to two different classes, distinguished by inequality in political power or in wealth. Slavery has been abolished in all parts of the world under the control of civilised powers, but in many places the legal machinery of contract is used to set up a system in which, under the name of indentured labour, all the characteristic features of slavery reappear. Even apart from the extreme evils of indentured labour the terms on which a 'free' bargain is concluded between a propertied employer and a propertyless employee tend inevitably, in the absence of legal or syndical safe-guards, unduly to favour the former. It is thus not entirely without justification that agitators refer to the lot of propertyless labourers under a system of free contract as 'wage-slavery'. Any form of economic and political pressure that acts more upon one side of the wage-contract than upon the other increases this tendency. Of forms of economic pressure two are important. One is purely economic; the necessity of mere existence. This acts in the case of persons who have no alternative means of liveli-hood except entering into such a contract, that is, chiefly, in the case of labourers in a society where the material means of production are nearly all owned by persons who are not labourers. Sometimes this economic necessity may be created by political means, as when common lands are enclosed or when upon the members of a hitherto self-sufficient tribe a tax is imposed so large that they must needs seek some source of income outside their own tribal grounds. The second kind of pressure is that of insistent legal obligation, chiefly debt. Very stringent laws of debt can make a debtor into something very like a slave, as both the Greeks and the Romans knew by experience. As will be shown later (Chapter IV, section 19) this form of pressure exists to-day, but it is masked under the form of productive capital.

Contract is a later developed juristic notion than Property, and in popular estimation contractual rights are held less 'sacred' than proprietary ones. Thus the fact that such rights are limited by considerations of general welfare is more generally admitted in the case of Contract than of Property. Hence come limitations of contract-rights, both in intensity and extensity, similar to those in the case of property, but more considerable in degree. The community, through the state, always reserves to itself the right of laying down conditions to which contracts must conform if they are to be held valid. Some states also assume the right of annulling contracts already entered into, if the public policy appears to require it.

Contract is associated with a fluid condition of property and with a flexible economic order: as Sir Henry Maine pointed out,[1] its importance is small in a society whose economic processes are chiefly regulated by the institution of Status and increases with economic freedom and economic rationality.[2] It is possible that it may outlast many forms of property: one can conceive of a socialistic

[1] *Ancient Law*, ch. 5, p. 151 (Tenth edition).
[2] By rationality is meant a conscious planning and directing of activities according to a deliberate calculation of ends and means. It is opposed to tradition, custom and unreflecting habit. (See p. 67.)

society in which all private property in production goods
(a very large category, indeed) had disappeared and yet
in which income actually accrued to individuals through
a network of contractual relationships.

23. Enough has been said to give an idea of the scope of
the institution of Property, including Inheritance and
Contract. For fuller treatment the reader must turn to the
work of Ely, just quoted, to Wagner's *Grundlegung* or to
Max Weber's *Wirtschaft und Gesellschaft*. It is, however,
worth while to recapitulate the ways in which modifications
of the form of the institution can effect the distribution of
wealth in a community, largely through restricting or
enlarging the opportunities of various categories of producers to earn a livelihood.

   1. With regard to the subject of ownership, the relative
extension of private property and public property, especially in the means of production, affects the size of individual incomes. Under private ownership there is always a
tendency, described more particularly in Chapter V,
pp. 173-176, for large incomes to pile themselves up; under
public ownership a part of the social dividend flows
through the hands of the organised community, thus
rendering possible a larger measure of social control of
income, which can be exercised, if desired, in the direction
of increasing equality.

   2. With regard to the object of ownership: we get
       (A) intensive limitation, and
       (B) extensive limitation of property-rights.
Under the first head we must mention the far-reaching
results of refusing altogether to recognise property-rights
in certain things, such as human beings, or to recognise
individual property-rights in such things as land, or
instruments of production in general.
   Under the second head come limitations on the exercise

of admitted rights, such as the prohibition of destruction or waste, the restriction in the rights of buying and selling certain commodities, the limitation of inheritance. Here also belong the imposition of conditions on ownership and contract. This is the direction at present taken by the most fruitful methods of social reform, such as the public control of public-utility concerns and the safeguarding of the worker's interest by hedging round the terms of the labour contract with various conditions—minimum wages, maximum hours, factory legislation, insurance and accident compensation—creating rights for the worker that he is legally unable to contract out of. These limitations and conditions are a potent, even if an indirect, method whereby society regulates the individual acquisition of income.

24. 3. STATUS.

Under this head are grouped a number of institutions that have to do with personal (including economic) freedom and unfreedom. All the social forces that tend to determine an individual's economic activity, by limiting his opportunities of earning a livelihood in some directions or by extending them in others, come under the heading of status. In proportion as tradition or social organisation limits his choice we say he is unfree. For, as an historical fact, unfreedom is the rule and freedom the exception. Periods in economic development occur wherein productive forces are unchained and individual self-expression comes into its own, but these are transient and transitional stages. Paramount social needs are always in the background, and the wild steed of individualism no sooner imagines that it has finally broken the hard rein than a fresh pull at its mouth proves to it that social necessity still has firm hold on the bridle. In our own day the nineteenth century's little gallop is drawing to a close. Men complain of enterprise being strangled in a net of bureaucratic regulations, but the same tendencies are at work in both private and public undertakings. The increasing complexity of modern economy is to blame; we may protest, but we cannot escape it.

25. When we speak of freedom we mean many things. Apart from metaphysical freedom (Freedom of the Will) we can have

    A. Freedom of Thought
    B. Freedom of Action
        1. Political Freedom (*a*) passive
                        (*b*) active
        2. Economic Freedom.

26. A. *Freedom of Thought.*—Economics is primarily concerned with men's overt acts, not with their secret thoughts. However, thought that is denied outward expression in words and opportunities of contact with other thoughts, can scarcely be said to be free. Freedom of thought requires, in order to fulfil itself, freedom of speech and printing, which are strictly speaking forms of political freedom. The connection between economics and freedom of thought and speech is not at once apparent. It is to be found, however, in the fact that intellectual activity refuses to be compartmentalised: a ban placed upon one form of speculative activity spreads to other forms and the restriction of liberty of thought in one department of life tends to sterilise all creative thought. Now the progress of economic society depends on the application of thought to technology and organisation. It is not therefore surprising that there exists in general a correlation between liberty of thought and economic progress. Thus the great burst of free intellectual activity in the eighteenth century known in France as 'philosophie' and in Germany as the 'Aufklärung', prepared the way for, if it did not actually stimulate, the great economic developments of the nineteenth century.

27. B.1. *Political Freedom.*—By passive political freedom is meant security and equality of civil rights, the reign of law and equal liberty of all citizens to do such things as the law, acting generally and impartially, does not forbid. By active political freedom is meant, in addition to passive political freedom, the right to take an equal part in the formation of laws and in the ultimate responsibility of government. In the definition of both kinds of political liberty, equality, in the sense of equality of rights (what the Greek thinkers designated 'isonomy'), is also postulated: this appears necessary since inequality of rights means a degree of political unfreedom for any persons whose rights are less extensive than those of others. The economic importance of political liberty and equality lies chiefly in the fact that human beings frequently regard it as a means to the acquisition of economic liberty and equality, and desire it or abhor it accordingly.

Thus the French bourgeoisie sought political rights in 1789 partly in order to win the economic rights of free enterprise, security, and access on equal terms to all land and all trades. In the European revolutionary movement of 1848 both bourgeoisie and proletariat demanded political rights from autocratic governments as a means of gaining economic rights. After the failure of the movement on the political side the former obtained, in most European countries, all that they really desired,,to wit, passive political liberty; while the latter continued the struggle for active political liberty in order to win economic rights (freedom of association, labour protection laws) as against the bourgeoisie rather than against the handful of soldiers and bureaucrats forming the autocracy. In fact the bourgeoisie now found an absolute government a welcome protector against working-class aggression and ceased to press with any energy the demand for active political freedom. In modern Europe the rightlessness of Jews and other national minorities in many countries is reflected in economic disadvantages such as exclusion from universities (and hence from the civil service and learned professions), lack of consideration in the framing of tariff policy, and unequal treatment under agrarian laws.

28. B.2. *Economic Freedom.*—In proportion as an individual is left free to choose and change his own avocation and to order his own activities within that avocation do we say he has economic freedom: there is personal mobility between different avocations. By economic freedom is frequently meant the absence of legal restrictions on any particular occupation and the absence of legal compulsion to do any particular economic act. But more than this is needed. The liberty to accept or refuse a sweated wage-contract with the alternative, in the event of refusal, of no wage-contract at all; the equal rights of the pauper and the millionaire to engage in any gainful occupation they think fit—these are not the full measure of economic liberty. The economic importance of freedom or un-freedom lies in the fact that limitations on the practice of an occupation by categories of persons tend to scarcen and therefore make dearer the services of persons permitted to follow that occupation to the detriment of all other persons. Those who are excluded have diminished earning power, so that inequality in economic opportunities is reflected in inequality of real incomes. As will be shown later (Chapter IV, p. 141, Chapter V, pp. 146–151), the most fundamental thing determining a person's economic position is his opportunity of earning. Just as political liberty implies equality of political rights, so does economic liberty imply equality of economic opportunity. An indi-

vidual may only be said to be economically free when he is free to choose any of the openings for which he is inherently physically or mentally qualified (this involves the opportunity to develop or acquire the necessary non-inherent qualifications) and to engage in it with as much chance of success as any other person with the same abilities. Under such conditions it can be proved that social welfare will be maximised and that every individual can, if he so choose, earn his maximum income, compatible with maximum social income.[1]

29. These conditions of economic freedom are absent under certain institutions, of which the chief are Class, Order and Caste. It is the position of a man with respect to these that is his Status. The last two are incompatible with political freedom. The first can coexist with political freedom, as has just been suggested. It is maintained, however, by other institutions, such as Property and Contract, that ultimately have political sanctions. All inequalities of economic opportunity are correlated with some coercive organisation of a political nature.

30. (a) *Class* consists in the existence among the population of a set of divisions according to economic wealth, the mobility between which is so small that there is not effective equality of economic opportunity between members of different divisions. The distinctions of Class are, however, not embodied in differences of formal legal rights and duties. Political liberty may guarantee a man equality of

---

[1] Marshall, *Principles of Economics*, V, ii, 1 (p. 331); V, xiii, 5 (p. 470). Pigou, *Economics of Welfare*, Pt. II, ch. ii and iii.

Professor Cannan remarks: 'If everyone could get free training for every profession, the costly ones would be over-supplied, because they would no longer bear their own complete cost—the services of the trainers would not be charged against the service. You could get over it by a system of taxation of the services.'

opportunity within the limits of his Class, but the force of accumulated wealth (inherited or earned) makes very unequal the chances of two individuals of different Classes of, say, starting a factory or practising a learned profession. Classes form non-competing groups (see Chapter V, sections 2–3).

31. (*b*) *Order* (in German *Stand*) is the term used here to denote differences of status formally imposed by law or custom having the force of law. The most familiar examples are to be found under the feudal system and in France and Germany between the end of the feudal system proper and the liberation of 1789–1848 (the *ancien régime*). The distinctions are usually hereditary, but in this case are not so unalterable as those of Caste; it is difficult but not as a rule impossible for a man to change his Order. Distinctions of Order involve, and are maintained by, differences in economic opportunity and in legal rights and obligations. Thus a noble or a peasant may not engage in trade; a merchant may not own land outside a town; peasants may not acquire nobles' land (or must make extra payments for the privilege) and nobles may not occupy peasants' holdings.

The most interesting order is that of Serfdom. A serf is a man who rents land on condition of rendering personal services, or in other words a labourer who is paid by the right to the use of a piece of land; he is personally unfree, geographically bound to the land, and unable to change his employer-landlord. As a rule, if and when the land changes ownership the serf changes his allegiance too: he follows the fortunes of the land.

32. The lowest position in a system of Orders is that of a slave. Slavery, the reduction of human beings to economic goods in which other people have exclusive property-rights, is the most complete negation of freedom. Even here, however, there are variations in the degree of extension admitted by society to the slave-owner's rights. Under some codes he might not kill, under others not even sell the slave. Frequently a slave had modified personal rights, even including those of owning personal property (in Roman law his *peculium*). A slave's peculium might even include another slave. A slave might engage in a gainful occupation for his own profit, but usually paid his owner a share of his earnings. Under some codes of law the child of a slave was a slave, under others every one was born free.

33. (c) *Caste* is an hereditary occupational group. The barriers of Caste are those of birth, not of wealth, but they may easily develop into divisions of wealth, for the products of some occupations are more in demand than others and thus the individuals following them, if their numbers do not increase at a greater rate than those in other occupations, may monopolise a large portion of the social dividend. How this occurs will be explained in Chapter V.

34. Akin to distinctions of Caste are distinctions based on race. Provided that miscegenation does not occur, or that, if it has occurred, it is kept within limits so that certain inter-racial mixtures are definitely segregated, races form perfect examples of non-competing groups (see p. 147). If different rates of pay are customarily paid to members of different races it is impossible for rates to be levelled by transference of individuals from one category to the other. The possibility that employers may substitute the labour of the lower-paid race for that of the higher-paid may tend to raise the pay of the former and lower that of the latter and so lessen the inequality. But such substitution cannot often go very far. Moreover, such substitution is possible only in a very indirect manner if discrimination be made between different occupations. If certain occupations are reserved for persons of certain races it will, as a rule, be easy to maintain considerable differences in earnings between occupations assigned to different races.

Thus any inequality in rights between races is likely to result in permanent and hereditary differences in economic opportunities. It is not particular occupations but groups of occupations that tend to become hereditary. One race has allotted to it the unskilled and ill-paid jobs, another monopolises the skilled and the best-paid. If a member of the superior race is required for unskilled work he can usually obtain the pay of a skilled man.

35. 4. THE FAMILY (including Marriage).

The family is a group of persons related by (usually near) kinship and bound by obligations of mutual support. Economically capable members of the family are bound to support economically incapable members. From the economic point of view the institution of the family serves two very important ends and one less important one. The first is that of assuring the support of children before they are capable of supporting themselves. The second is that of assuring the support of women while they are occupied in bearing and rearing children. The third, biologically and socially less indispensable, end is that of assuring the support of adults in sickness and in old age.[1]

The simplest form of the family, occurring in the most primitive as well as in the most advanced communities, is the group of one man, one woman and the woman's children. The man is bound to support the woman and her children; the woman also contributes according to her

---

[1] Also during unemployment, where the economic structure of society involves periods of involuntary and uncompensated idleness.

ability. Other kinds of family are possible: several men may jointly support one woman and her children (polyandry); one man may support several women and their children (polygyny); several units of man, woman and children, usually descendants of a single couple, may live together and support one another (the joint family). It is not necessary that the men should be the women's husbands or even the fathers of their children: in some cases the men are the women's brothers and the economic obligations of the husband are not to his wife but to his sisters.

Owing to the fact that usually the sexes are approximately equal in number, the family tends always towards the monogamic group of father, mother and children. When polygamy occurs it usually upsets the distribution of the sexes in the family group that would naturally occur according to the sex ratio of the community as a whole. Thus polygamy (especially in the form of polygyny) is in most cases the perquisite of the dominant class. This may be brought about in two opposite ways. Where, as among the pastoral African peoples, a wife produces wealth for her husband, a man who has many wives has a large investment in means of production: he is rich because he has many wives. On the other hand, among more advanced peoples practising polygamy the possession of a wife involves much expense and only the rich can afford more than one: he has many wives because he is rich.

36. Marriage is the social institution that regulates the permanent union of the sexes. In communities which do not recognise the fact of paternity, the marriage relation cuts across the family relation, and disturbs the symmetry of the social grouping on lines of kinship, but in most human societies, Marriage and the Family are closely welded into one institution and the personal and sexual aspect of the former tends to be smothered under the economic pre-occupations of the latter.

37. Since the family is an economic association containing individuals of both sexes, it is closely bound up with the economic differentiations of the sexes (division of labour between men and women). Since difference of function usually leads to difference of status and difference of status to inequality of status, the institution of the Family is connected with the economic inequality of the sexes.

With the development of economic rationality and economic individualism the typical form of the family relationship becomes the responsibility of one man for the support of his wife and children.

Within the monogamous family-unit the economic relations between the husband and the wife depend on the relative importance of their respective contributions to the family livelihood, and may vary from complete dependence of the wife on the husband, in communities where the woman's part of the division of labour is quite unimportant, through practical economic equality, to partial dependence of the husband on the wife, found in a few communities where women's functions are the more important.[1] Thus, under the division of labour usual in primitive communities that assigns the chase to men and agriculture to women, women's place in the community depends on the importance of agriculture relative to hunting. From hunting to fighting is a short cry, and the importance of war and the warrior in society appears to be inversely correlated with that of women. Owing to the fact that one of women's functions, child-bearing and child-rearing, has

[1] It is a case of relative elasticities of demand (reciprocal demand) between two perfect non-competing groups. (See Chapter IV, pp. 113–114.)

See also Pigou, *Economics of Welfare*, Pt. III, ch. xiii, § 9, and M. and M. Vaerting, *The Dominant Sex*.

no immediate economic value and has to be performed either as a spare-time hobby or else as a personal service rendered to the father, the scales are always slightly tilted in women's disfavour. In a rationalised and individualised society these economic differences are reflected in differences of personal income and are transmitted, by the influence of competition, from wives to women in general. Although in some occupations women are, in general, more efficient than men, the marginal woman's labour is less in demand than the marginal man's. Thus a level is set for the basic wages of each sex. These are the chief factors influencing the incomes of men and women in modern civilisation. The position of woman in the home and outside the home cannot be considered as two separate questions but form one problem. Men and women, being easily distinguished by their appearance, form two perfect non-competing groups and the distribution of the social income between them follows the laws of international trade.

When sexual intercourse itself comes to acquire an economic value, the under-valued sex finds a commodity, the sale of which may help to redress the balance. However, there is no room here to discuss the economics of Prostitution. It is not probable that this latter institution, the stepsister of Marriage, much affects the division of income between men and women.[1]

38. Men and women are two sexes of one species and not two separate species, as many writers seem to think. Hence the differentiation in function and economic status does not persist beyond the lifetime of the person. No permanent division into classes, castes or orders can follow from the unequal opportunities of the sexes. Where such a division, based on other grounds, already occurs, the

[1] See Dalton, *Inequality of Incomes*, p. 260.

usual tendency of people to mate within their own rank (which is frequently stereotyped by custom and even by positive law) tends to perpetuate these differences.[1] A curious case, however, occurs in some Indian castes, where hypergamy or hypogamy prevails, that is the obligation of a man to take his wife from a higher or from a lower subdivision of the caste than his own, the caste being divided according to wealth and position. This, coupled with a well-developed system of property, leads to an elaborate system of dowries for either sons or daughters according to the end of the scale that is least sought after, which dowries are sometimes so large as practically to ruin a family. Hypogamy is not uncommon. Where the importance of fighting or other causes have raised the position of men and lowered that of women to the category of property, the men of a dominant group will take women from an inferior group but refuse to give their women to men of a lower group. Hence the importance of the right of *connubium* in the eyes of the Roman plebs.

Under the modern individualistic monogamy referred to above, society tries to assure the support of wife and children through a sub-contract, so to speak, with the husband. One important result of this is that the income of a child varies directly as that of its father and inversely as the number of persons in the family. This means that parents transmit a large part of the economic advantages or disadvantages of their position to their offspring. If the birthrate is the same in all classes, the relative economic position of different classes will remain unaltered.[2] If there is a differential birthrate (as in most countries nowadays)

[1] See Dalton, *Inequality of Incomes*, pp. 307–308.
[2] It may be that the rich, being able to give their children better conditions, will raise more children to men's and women's estate than the poor: the consequent provision of a start in life to sons and of marriage portions to daughters will tend, especially where the practice of equal division of the family fortune among children

in the sense that the wealthier parents have the fewer children, there are fewer children to share the larger family incomes and the existing inequality of incomes will be augmented. Another consequence of a differential birth-rate, important to the eugenist if not to the economist, is that when people are better-off and therefore more able to provide a favourable environment for the rising genera-tion, they have a stronger direct economic incentive to limit their family. Hence the poorest homes make more than their proportionate contribution to the rising genera-tion. Also, in a régime of economic freedom the well-to-do contain a certain proportion of more efficient persons promoted from below; thus efficiency tends to be asso-ciated with diminished fertility. Hence the compara-tive sterility of the leisured class and the 'proliferation from below' that so much troubles some of our Christian sociologists.[1]

39. 5. EDUCATION.

Education is the process through which individuals pass before finally taking their place as component parts of society and which fits them for the position they are destined to hold in that society.

This refers primarily to what Bernard Shaw calls 'technical', i.e. utilitarian and vocational (professional) education, but it also refers to 'humane' education, since general culture is part of an individual's social functions.

is observed, to reduce the average wealth per head of the rich. If the rich do not form a definite class but are merely those individuals who enjoy better luck or are more gifted than the common man, this force will tend to re-establish equality from generation to genera-tion. If, however, the rich owe their wealth to class advantages involving privilege and inequality of opportunity, this force will do little to mitigate inequality and there will be a tendency for the inequality of the parents' position to be perpetuated in the children's.

[1] W. R. Inge, *Christian Ethics and Modern Problems* (1930), p. 269.

As economists, however, we are only concerned here with utilitarian education. This falls into two parts:—

(1) That which prepares the individual generally for membership of society and of a given community with its traditions, customs and ethos.

(2) That which prepares him for his particular part, as member of a particular class, caste or rank, as a producer and a consumer. This includes vocational and technical education in the narrower sense.

From a consideration of the function of Education it is obvious that any particular structure of society as regards status must be related to a particular kind of education. A slave will receive a slave's upbringing and a noble a noble's upbringing. A class society connotes class education.

40. From the economic point of view three aspects of an educational system are important:—

(i) The nature of the education itself, its economic value, and its efficiency for its particular purpose. The educational system of a country can be, even more than its state organisation and its industrial organisation, its most valuable economic asset, e.g. the value to Germany of the technical education of its young people during the years after 1871. It is one of the most important of List's 'productive powers'.

(ii) The degree to which it stereotypes already existing class or caste divisions, or, on the other hand, tends towards greater economic mobility.

(iii) The financing of education, whether at private or at the public cost. The provision of free and equal training is one of the most potent of influences destroying class or professional monopolies, just as the making of education into a competitive commodity, of which the longest purse can purchase most, is one of the most effective means by which, through hindering mobility, inequalities of opportunity are maintained.

41. Education is changing rapidly, in our own days, from an individualistic function, privately financed, to a socialistic one, collectively financed. In the course of this process the community in its collective capacity is assuming more and more responsibility for the health, support and welfare of the child, so that Education is beginning to trench on the functions of the Family. If the advocates of mothers' pensions and family endowment have their way, or, still more, if some kind of socialistic order comes into being, the Family will have lost its chief economic functions and will be restricted in scope to the regulation of personal relations. It is possible that Marriage will then re-acquire another function, that it has had in other times and places but has lost in our Occidental culture, to wit the regulation of the number of the population. Putting this possibility aside, these two functions of the Family, the economic and the non-economic, will be provided for by two distinct institutions. The Family will then have lost its social character; it will have become, like religion, 'de-institutionalised' or a matter for individual preference and not for social control. It will become a purely personal thing, a centre of affective relationships of individuals. That we are nowadays moving in this direction it is difficult to doubt.

42. 6. RELIGION.

Although, considered as a social institution, Religion is nowadays but an attenuated ghost of its former self, its enormous importance to the individual shows what social value it once had. The purely economic significance of religion may be considered under two heads: its direct influence and its indirect influence on economic activity.

43. (i) The direct economic influence of Religion is greatest in the earlier stages of social development when religion or magic was intimately bound up with food-getting technique, that is to say, when magical or religious practices were believed to affect the supply of food animals or the growth of crops. Examples of this are the sympathetic magic embodied in totemic ceremonies; the crop-magic and fertility rituals of the early agricultural peoples; and the priestly regulation of the chief operations of the agricultural year, developing into priestly control of the calendar. Long after agriculture and the chase had become secularised in technique, priestly castes continued to draw from the community, in the form of tithes, first-fruits and other dues, payment for services that were originally thought to be productive but had long since become petrified into mere ceremonial. The clergy then stood alongside the nobility as one of the superior orders of a stratified society and tithes became a form of income akin to taxes and feudal dues.

44. (ii) The indirect economic influence of Religion is much more far-reaching. It occurs in the form of intimate connections between religion and other social institutions. Such connections are manifold and pervasive. We see them for instance (*a*) when Religion acts as a buttress to some other institutions; (*b*) when Religion becomes embodied in corporations that own and manage property and may undertake material production; or (*c*) more subtly, when Religion becomes associated with some ethical code that sanctions forms of conduct that have more or less economic value.

(*a*) Religion, having its psychological roots in the more primitive layers of man's being, tends to be a conservative force. This tendency is augmented when religion takes an 'institutional' form, that is when its human agents are organised into castes or corporations and when these castes or corporations acquire property and political power. Thus religion is admirably suited to be the prop and mainstay of whatever other institutions of Property, Status and the Family may exist at the moment. In India, the ultimate sanction of the caste system is religious. In the United States of America, before 1865, organised religion supported the institution of slavery. It has been said that the Methodist Revival was the chief means of sheltering the arrangements regarding Class and Property of eighteenth-century England from the storm that shattered those of eighteenth-century France. It is generally recognised that Religion is the great preservative force that maintains the social norms of the Family, especially in its aspect of regulated sex-relationship, and, to a lesser degree, of Education.

(b) Another kind of connection between Religion and Property is exemplified by the activity of religious corporations as owners of property or undertakers of industry. The temple-treasuries of Mesopotamia and Greece carried out extensive banking and exchange transactions and were centres to which merchants and private brokers gravitated. The temples of Egypt at one time not only owned much of the land and cultivated it with their serfs but provisioned the kingdom from their granaries and provided by their treasuries a banking system for the financial needs of the state. In Muhammadan countries the wakf or religious endowment developed into a form of land tenure that enjoyed comparative security even under the anarchy of the Turk and of the petty despots of Islam's decadence. But the most familiar example of this connection is the monastic establishments of Western Europe. During the middle ages the monasteries introduced improved methods of cultivation and developed the useful arts. Favoured by the privileges (such as exemption from certain taxes and from military service) that their religious functions earned

for them and enjoying the advantages of corporate existence and perpetual succession, they increased in wealth and
power. No heir dissipated their accumulated treasure or
mortgaged their extended domains: on the contrary, into
their hands fell the lands of improvident kinghts and
extravagant kings. Corporations themselves, they could
compete in toughness of purpose and length of foresight
with corporations of burgesses and, while needy secular
lords bartered for present grants the future increments of
their cities, the monasteries rarely gave charters of freedom
to the townsfolk in their domain. Their serfs they treated
as a rule without brutality, but they exacted their customary
rights to the full. They enfranchised their serfs in most
cases later than the lay lords.

(c) In a more subtle manner Religion is an economic
force when it becomes associated with certain moral ideals
bearing on economic conduct and lends to them its mighty
psychological force. Thus we may not unfairly attribute
the over-population of India and China in part to religions
that make the begetting of children a moral duty. Religious
prohibition of certain foods or drinks may have an influence
on the physique and morale of a people and hence on its
economic efficiency. The effect on economic development
of the medieval Church's prohibition of usury may be
exaggerated in the popular mind, but it undoubtedly
existed. The same may be said for the effect of Protes-
tantism (especially in its Calvinistic form) on economic
life. To the Puritan, wealth was not an evil in itself, but it
was to be regarded as a trust and not as a means to carnal
enjoyment. As a trust, it was to be managed diligently
and prudently. Hence the making of money became a
moral good and the spending of it an evil. In this way
saving was forced upon the Puritan, greatly to the advantage of the class of trading and manufacturing burghers
to which he characteristically belonged.

45. In modern times the part played by Religion in social and economic life is much diminished. Socially, Religion is escaping from collective control and becoming a purely personal matter: in other words it is ceasing to be a social institution at all. Economically, while its direct influence as a condition of material production is practically extinct, its indirect influence as a bulwark of other institutions and its influence through religious corporations in their capacity as property owners is declining with the decline of religion as an organised social institution. There is left the indirect influence of Religion through ethical standards. Thus, at the present day, the attitude of certain religious bodies to contraception and to practical eugenics is one of the greatest obstacles to rational social control of the population. With the decline of the power and influence of organised religious corporations, Religion, while it remains psychologically conservative, has a chance of becoming politically liberal. Hence the frequent coalescence of sincere religious thought with such movements as internationalism and pacifism and the more socialistic tendencies of social reform (or the more reformist tendencies of socialism). If the influence of organised religion were used to advocate the ethics of the New Testament, changes of incalculable consequence would be introduced into all our economic institutions. However, it is probable that the de-institutionalising of Religion is weakening its ethical driving power. In former times the great strength of Religion lay in the fact that it was the embodiment of the conscience of society: its ethical precepts might be irrational, but they had the emotional force of collective opinion behind them. Now that Religion is a private matter, its ethical precepts are based more on purely individual thought and feeling; while they are in general more rational they have lost the compelling power that comes from the voice of the herd.

CHAPTER III

THEORY OF VALUE

1. The analysis of Value falls into two parts, corresponding to two senses in which the word can be used. In the first place Value may mean a purely individual and subjective relation of a thing (called a good) to a person. In the second place it may mean the social relations of a good to a community of people. In the social order with which we have to do this relation emerges through the process of exchange in the market and is thus called Exchange-Value. The second is derived from the first and its analysis is dependent on that of the first.

The analysis of Use-Value is valid for all possible conditions of a rational being dealing with material things: for an isolated individual like Robinson Crusoe, for a self-supporting household or for a completely communistic community, as well as for the individual units of a society using money and exchange. The analysis of Exchange-Value is valid only for a particular range of societies with certain institutions. These institutions are usually taken to be economic freedom, private property, individual enterprise, and exchange in a free market with the use of some form of money. It will, however, be valid for a régime of collective enterprise and public property in means of production, provided that there is private property in consumption goods, exchange of such goods on a market, money (in the sense of dispensable purchasing power), and economic freedom for ultimate consumers and ultimate producers (wage-earners employed by the community).

2. 1. Use-Value

Need is the origin of Value. Needs may or may not require for their satisfaction the exclusive control and disposal of material objects, personal services or socially guaranteed relations ('rights'). All these things may be called goods, material or immaterial. Needs that do not require such exclusive control do not enter into the realm of economics. If they do they may be termed economic needs. Again economic needs may or may not depend for their satisfaction on disposal over definite individual goods. If they do not—if, that is to say, the quantity of goods available is great enough to satisfy the need entirely and still leave some goods over—the goods are non-economic goods. If the goods, however, are scarce, in the sense that they are insufficient for the complete satisfaction of need, then any partial satisfaction of need is dependent on disposal over particular goods. If one of the goods is lost, some satisfaction is lost. Under these circumstances the goods are economic goods. An economic good derives its value (use-value) from the satisfaction that is dependent on it and the greater the satisfaction the higher is the value of the good.

3. If only a single good is under consideration its importance to the user measures its use-value. If a person disposes of a number of similar goods during a given period of time, he is said to have a supply of such a number. Now the goods composing a supply satisfy different needs and might therefore be expected to have different values. But since they are substitutes for one another each good will be estimated by the user at the same value. Also, since the loss of one good out of the supply entails the loss of the least important satisfaction of those covered by the supply, the use-value of one good is measured by the importance of this least important satisfaction. The least important need satisfied is often called the marginal need and the good that satisfies it the marginal good. Thus the use-value of each good in a supply is that of the marginal good and is measured by the least important need satisfied. The use-value of the whole supply is the product of the number of goods into the use-value of the marginal good. As the supply increases, the marginal need represents a less degree of satisfaction and consequently the value of the marginal good declines with increasing supply.

The quality of yielding satisfaction is frequently called utility—other proposed names are 'desiredness'[1] and 'ophelimity'.[2] The utility of the marginal good is called the marginal utility of the supply and the relation established above between quantity supplied and use-value is called the law of diminishing marginal utility. The sum of the needs that are satisfied by a given supply is the measure of the total utility of the supply. But since the supply is valued by marginal utility and not by total utility, the latter concept is of little importance in the theory of value.

The marginal good is often spoken of as the last good of the supply, but this is misleading, since no particular individual good is marginal. Any good is marginal: it is merely the one that makes the difference between a given supply and the same supply increased by an additional unit. If the stock is large, then the additional one good can be considered as an infinitesimal increment, and the marginal utility becomes the differential of the total utility with respect to the quantity of the good. For the present we may regard the marginal good as a finite increment: later, in the discussion of value-determination in an organised market wherein the demand of a large number of persons becomes effective, the assumption in the typical

[1] A. C. Pigou, *Economics of Welfare*, Bk. I, Ch. ii, § 1.
[2] V. Pareto, *Cours d'Économie Politique*, § 5.

case of an infinitely small increment becomes justified and is the foundation of the mathematical theory of value.

4. It is necessary now to introduce a new assumption that is less well grounded than the previous one and that introduces at the outset a somewhat arbitrary element into economics. This is the assumption that, in the individual economy that we are considering, economic activities are rationally directed. That is to say that the individual consciously seeks to increase his income of utilities by procuring more of the goods that experience teaches him yield utility, by procuring them with the least sacrifice of other utilities, and by using them in such a way as to extract the most utility from them: this involves some amount of experiment, trial and error, learning from experience, conscious assumption of certain gratifications as ends, and deliberate adaptation of means to ends. This assumption need not appear so alarmingly artificial and over-simplified if we realise three things. One is that it is not necessary to assume a complete rationalisation of effort; a mere tendency in this direction is sufficient to validate the following arguments. The second is that if we include ethical and sentimental gratifications in our measuring and balancing of utilities, we are including a great many cases that at first sight seem to be exceptions to our assumptions. In fact, if we push the objective method to its logical conclusion we must assume that wherever a man prefers one course of action to another, the first has higher utility—this is the objective definition of utility. A given individual's judgments of utility approximate to those of the traditional 'economic man' in proportion as he is adapted to an industrial civilisation. The third thing is that even in the cases where rationality seems most absent, to wit, in traditional methods of production and customary forms of consumption, they must have possessed

some survival value to have become customary and hence embody collective (perhaps unconscious) experience and adaptation of means to ends.

5. If people like a thing they try to get more of it. If goods are present in sufficient quantity a man will supply himself with them until their marginal utility sinks to zero. In this case their Use-Value also vanishes and the goods themselves disappear from the purview of value-theory. If the supply be still further increased, the marginal utility may become negative, that is, the good will have a negative value, it is an encumbrance that one wishes to get rid of.

In most cases there is no need to have more. Supply ceases when value no longer exists. This is the case with so-called free goods, i.e. goods that can be obtained from nature for the taking. Hence the paradox that a good may be an undoubted good, useful and desired, but may have little value, while another good may satisfy much less urgent desires and yet have high value, e.g. bread and diamonds. The first has great total utility but low marginal utility; the second has lesser total utility, but it has a high marginal utility.

If nature is less generous with a good, that is, if it is scarce, everyone cannot have enough of it and so its marginal utility never sinks to zero. It thus retains some Use-Value and is an economic good. (Such goods are usually called commodities, but this term is best restricted to goods produced for sale in a market. In what follows they will be called simply goods, free goods being referred to, when it is necessary to mention them, as non-economic goods.)

Scarcity is then the condition for the emergence of value, but not the cause of value. The interrelation of those two hoary monsters, the Gog and Magog of economics, Supply and Demand, is now seen. Demand, working through utility and marginal utility, is the cause of value in general. Demand, by determining the degree of marginal utility corresponding to any given quantity of the good, is one of the determinants of its actual value in a particular case; Supply, or the degree of scarcity, by defining the actual quantity and hence in determining the level of marginal utility in the case of the particular good, is the other determinant of value in a particular case. With a given set of satisfactions depending on the existence of various quantities of a good, the degree of scarcity determines the particular point at which the fall of value is arrested. With a determinate supply of a good, the urgency of the various needs whose satisfaction depends on disposal over it will determine the value of the marginal unit. A high degree of scarcity or a high intensity of need mean high value: a low degree of scarcity (relative abundance) or a low intensity of need mean low value.

6. We have now, still confining ourselves to individual subjective calculations, to discuss a case which becomes of increasing importance as society becomes more complex. There are many objects that are desired not as ends, themselves yielding their possessor some gratification, but as means for the procuring of other objects that are wanted for their own sake. Even in an economy that knows no sale or barter, such as individual production and consumption or the housekeeping of a family or of a community that produces only for use, there are raw materials and instruments of production. Goods that are sources of immediate satisfaction are called by Menger goods of the first order, goods used in the making of them are called goods of the second order, those used in the making of second order goods are called goods of the third order, and so on. In general, all goods of order above the first are called goods of higher order. These have value because of the value of their products: part of the value of the end product is reflected on to them, their value is derived or imputed. This process of imputation of value is important: it lies at the base of the theory of the value of factors of production and of rent. It is plain that, at any rate in the realm of individual subjective valuation, a good of higher order does not give value to the good of lower order into which it enters, but receives value from it. The law of diminishing marginal utility applies to higher order goods as to those of the first order, not only as a direct result of the diminishing marginal utility of the goods into which they enter, but in addition because of technical considerations (law of diminishing returns—see section 30).

7. The simplest case of imputed value is where a good passes directly into one of lower order, without the co-operation of any other goods and without having any alternative use. Here it is plain that the whole value of the product is imputed to it. A more complicated case is where a production-good enters into many finished products: it is then in demand from as many different quarters. This is a case of composite demand. Or several different higher-order goods may require to be combined in the production of one good of the first order. This is a case of joint demand. The use-value of goods in composite demand will be considered in the following section. That of goods in joint demand, although of great theoretical interest, is not essential to the present argument and will therefore be omitted. The exchange-value of goods in joint demand is, however, fundamental in the theory of distribution and will be discussed in detail later (section 29).

8. A good in composite demand acquires a value from each of the uses to which it can be put, but only one can be the value of the good. Obviously, in the same way as the value of each one of a stock of goods is derived from the marginal good, so the value of a compositely-demanded good will be the value that it acquires from its marginal use. Now if a unit is removed from the stock, the use from which it will be withdrawn will be that yielding the least utility; hence the marginal use is that from which the good acquires the least value, and it is this lowest value which is the actual value of the good in question. A man disposing of such a good will, if he directs his economy rationally, so apportion it between different uses as to make its marginal utility equal in all; that is to say, its value in all uses coincides with its marginal value. In individual economy this cannot always be done, either from the fact that the good cannot be split up into units sufficiently small, or from lack of rationality (ignorance, laziness, deadweight of tradition, etc.).

9. The concept of cost must now be mentioned. Two kinds of costs exist. In the first place, the actual efforts involved in the production of a given article are often felt as a burden. Just as the desirability of any good diminishes as one has more of it, until its marginal utility becomes zero and ultimately negative, so the desirability of work dwindles to zero and soon becomes negative. The first part of a spell of work may be pleasurable, a point of indifference is then reached, and after a certain point (in some cases from the very beginning) it becomes a toil and a pain. In general the disutility of a unit of work increases as the quantity of work increases. Hence we may reckon the cost of a good as measured by the marginal disutility of its production, just as we measured its value by the marginal utility of its consumption.

In the second place, however, we may think of the cost of a good in terms of the opportunities of obtaining other gratifications forgone in the making of it. Time and energy are limited: that which is spent in one activity cannot be spent on another. According to the conception of disutility-cost, a boy picking blackberries stops when the enjoyment of eating one blackberry has sunk so low that it only just compensates the fatigue of picking it. Very often, however, he stops, with an appetite for black-berries still lively and no consciousness of effort involved in the picking of them, simply because climbing a tree or jumping a ditch offers a richer return of enjoyment for the time and energy expended. This kind of cost is termed opportunity-cost, and, as will be seen later (section 31), importance in the consideration of production for a market. Since a rational economic subject will not give up one activity in favour of another one yielding less utility, the yield of utility of whatever he is actually engaged upon must be just greater than that of the most utility-yielding of the activities he is forgoing. Thus the opportunity-cost is measured by the marginal utility of the opportunity of highest utility that is given up. Hence we are justified in treating opportunity-cost as a particular case of value. But of the two kinds of cost, which is decisive in determining the cost of a good? The answer is, whichever is the higher, the marginal disutility of effort or the marginal utility of the opportunity forgone. The cost of gathering blackberries in the example just given, is not the pain of picking, but the renounced enjoyment of jumping or climbing.

10. The idea of cost can be extended. If a good is used for the production of another good, the possibility of any other use is thereby lost, and so the marginal utility of the next possible use is the same as the opportunity-cost. Thus arises the common concept of cost of production as the value of the higher-order goods used up in production.

Now there are some goods entering into the formation

of nearly all consumption-goods: they are in both composite and joint demand. These it is proposed to call
cost-goods, their values are costs. (Wieser calls the goods
themselves costs and uses the term cost-goods to denote
goods produced under conditions where cost is equal to
marginal utility: our unrestricted goods, cf. section 34.)

11. Throughout the process of individual valuation a kind of
balancing goes on. The relative advantages of alternative
uses of goods or alternative uses of time are weighed and
compared. Wherever one good can be transferred from one
employment where the utility of the marginal unit is low
to one where it is higher, a gain in total utility results:
hence the optimum utilisation of resources is that which
equalises their marginal utility in all employments. Thus
marginal utility becomes the criterion of the effective use
of resources. Underneath the whole process of valuation
and costing and all the intricacies of imputed value, of
composite and of joint demand, lies the principle of
balancing alternative uses and of equalising marginal
utilities.

12. It may be objected that the above analysis is too fine-
spun, that it makes assumptions doubtful in psychology,
and out of place in economics. Cassel[1] wishes to reject it
altogether, starting the theory of value at the stage of
Exchange-Value or Price; in his system, scarcity takes the
place of utility in ours, but the subsequent working out of
the laws of price formation, the pricing of factors of
production and the rest of the theory of value, cost and
distribution is the same as in our system. However, the
inquiring mind wishes to go behind the mere fact of a rise
in demand price with increasing scarcity and the utility
theory agrees fairly well with the facts whether it is

[1] G. Cassel, *Theory of Social Economy*, p. 80 (1932 edition).

considered introspectively or behaviouristically. The law of diminishing marginal utility reminds one of the psycho-physiological phenomenon of diminishing response to repeated stimuli.

The psychological analysis has the advantage of emphasising the part played by demand in the determination of value. Value is derived from demand, and demand from desire: the utility theory makes some attempt to take this desire into account. It should surely be otiose to repeat that value is derived from demand and not from either labour or sacrifice. It may be that effort is expended on things because they are valuable, but they do not become valuable because they cost effort. Similarly, people do not receive income for working or for saving or for owning because of the costs or the deserts involved therein, but because there happens to be a demand for the products of working or saving or for the use of the thing owned. In these days, however, of safeguarding and state-aided cartels, in which producers' interests take precedence of consumers' (when producers are powerful enough) and in which the fact that business men have sunk capital in an undertaking is considered as giving them a prescriptive right to extract profits from it, it may not be unnecessary to reiterate these elementary but fundamental principles of the economic life of society.

13. 2. EXCHANGE-VALUE

The second step in the elucidation of value is to introduce the idea of exchange, which leads ultimately to those of price and of an organised market. An individual, as well as disposing of his own resources, has now, indirectly, a control over those of the whole community in which he lives. In order to procure for himself utilities he has not only the method of making use of his own resources and his own efforts for their immediate production, but has the further method of using these resources and efforts for the production of goods which, even if he does not desire them himself, may be exchanged with other people against goods that he does desire. These goods, produced for exchange and not for personal use, are, for him, goods of the second order and only have value imputed to them for what they will fetch in exchange. But in order to be exchangeable they must be desired by someone, for whom they are either goods of the first order or goods destined for the production of such. That is to say, Use-Value is the origin of Exchange-Value. How the latter category is derived from the first will be considered in section 14.

But first it must be observed that in introducing exchange we have introduced society and social institutions. The process we are going to examine is no longer individual valuation and costing, but social valuation and costing. The terms 'subjective' and 'objective' used in the phrases 'subjective use-value', 'subjective exchange-value', and 'objective exchange-value' might be replaced by 'individual' and 'social'. As soon as society comes into consideration so do institutions. Barter or sale are themselves institutions; they rest on another institution, private property. A market of any sort, including a free market, is an institution. There are, however, other ways that can be thought of and that have occurred in history of integrating individual economic activity into a social whole. There is, for instance, the family or tribal economy, which, when enlarged, passes into the form of communistic community that has only collective property and produces for use only, not for exchange, and that regulates consumption by the force of collective opinion. There is also the slave community in which many work under the stimulus of force and fear to enrich one master, who distributes to them by his mere fiat what he thinks necessary for their existence. The historical importance of the price-and-market method lies in the fact that it is the most supple and adaptable, making possible the improvement of technique and the extension of scale. It has the convenience of effecting the best synthesis of two things that in other systems are incompatible: social co-operation on a large scale in production and individual choice over a wide range in consumption. But it must not be forgotten that we are now dealing with institutions, and that the phenomena of price and markets, capital and interest, wages and rent that are to be discussed are not of permanent validity, like the technical conditions of production and the psychological processes of subjective valuation, but are historical categories, in the phrase of the German historical school, and in a constant state of change and development.

14. As soon as it is possible to procure goods by exchange, a good acquires a new value, its exchange-value. A man is benefited by exchanging a good in his possession against another that he desires to obtain, if the use-value of the latter is just greater than the use-value of the former. The use-value of a good in exchange may be called its subjective or individual exchange-value. The term may be applied both to the good desired and to the good offered for it. This subjective exchange-value depends on two factors, on the use-value of the good demanded, and on the use-value of the good offered in exchange. But as soon as exchange becomes general, i.e. with the creation of a market, any good may be offered in exchange to obtain, either directly or through intermediate transactions, the good desired. Thus we must introduce two new conceptions: that of a commodity and that of purchasing power.

15. A commodity is a good produced for exchange.[1] For the

[1] This is the usual German use of the word. Menger defines a commodity as 'an economic good destined for exchange'. Most English

producer or seller it is a higher-order good. For the ultimate buyer it is a first-order good: in his hands it ceases to be a commodity, but remains a good. Purchasing power consists of a stock of goods disposable in exchange. They are used to obtain commodities and are always, in their holders' hands, higher-order goods. These two terms, commodities and purchasing power, are correlatives: purchasing power buys commodities, commodities are sold for purchasing power.

Any good disposable in exchange is a good with many uses, i.e. a good in composite demand. Its subjective use-value as a good and its subjective exchange-values in different transactions are examples of the values in different uses of a good in composite demand. These different values tend to equality.

Since no one will offer a good in exchange for a desired object unless the use-value of the good offered is no higher than that of any other good disposable in exchange, the use-value of the good offered in exchange becomes identical with the use-value of purchasing power in general.

16. A rational economic subject will allocate the resources at his disposal so as to obtain the same use-value from the marginal unit of purchasing power laid out in the acquisition of each different kind of commodity. For, if this is not so, the subject can increase his economic well-being by transferring purchasing power from the acquisition of those goods that yield less satisfaction at the margin (thereby increasing their marginal utility) to the acquisition

writers, however, use it as a general term for 'goods and services': here we use the word 'good' in this extended sense and obtain the convenient distinction between a 'good', which may or may not be produced for the market, and a 'commodity', which is so produced. Goods definitely not produced for exchange we may call 'goods produced for producer's own consumption'.

of those goods that yield more satisfaction (thereby lowering their marginal utility) until all goods have equal marginal utility per unit of outlay (the 'shillingsworth'), when further transferences will no longer increase, but will in fact diminish, economic well-being. (This is sometimes called the law of equi-marginal satisfaction.) As in the case of marginal utility of a single good, it is not necessary to assume perfect rationality. It will be seen that with ordinary economic subjects there is a tendency towards equi-marginal satisfaction. Even to perfectly rational subjects this process is only possible in the case of commodities the quantity of which can be varied by small increments; it cannot be applied to those that enter as unique wholes into the ordinary range of consumption. Thus it is applicable to things like bread, beer and bacon, but not to things like pianos and motor-cars. There is, however, a choice between articles of different size and quality. Thus even in the case of these 'singletons' there is a rough adjustment of the scale of consumption to the marginal utilities of other branches of expenditure.

Since the value of the marginal 'shillingsworths' of the innumerable different commodities purchased are equal to each other, and since the marginal utility of any particular quantity of purchasing power is derived from that of the commodity that this quantity is used to acquire, it follows that there is a marginal utility of purchasing power in general, corresponding to the general level of satisfaction that it enables its possessor to attain. We can now define an economic subject's supply of purchasing power during a given period as his income during that period. What holds good of commodities in particular holds good of purchasing power in general: the marginal utility of income falls off as the income increases. Put in less technical terms, the expenditure of a shilling by a well-off man satisfies much less urgent needs than that of a shilling by a poor man.

This is sometimes called the law of the diminishing marginal utility of income.

17. The more a good is desired the more will a man be ready to sacrifice in order to possess it: hence the subjective exchange-value of a good varies directly with its use-value. The more income is desired the less of it will a man be ready to sacrifice in order to obtain a given satisfaction: hence the subjective exchange-value of goods in general varies inversely with the use-value (marginal utility) of income. By the mathematical method (assuming infinitesimal increments) it can be shown that

$$\text{Subjective exchange-value} = \frac{\text{use-value of good}}{\text{use-value of income}}$$

The reciprocal of the use-value of income acts as a constant factor by which a man multiplies his whole scale of use-values of goods when he bids for commodities in the market. Thus, in the process by which subjective exchange-values are derived from subjective use-values, inequalities in the distribution of income introduce a systematic perversion or distortion into the measurement of human needs, which distortion extends to the whole of the subsequently derived apparatus of price and cost. (See footnote to p. 86.)

18. But we have not yet laid bare the mechanism of price. We have found out what a man is ready to offer for a good, but do not know whether he will get it at all, or, whether if he does, it will be for the most he will offer or for less. We must investigate price-formation in a market.

The essential characteristic of a market is the existence of a uniform exchange-value for any given good at a given moment. That is, we have an objective exchange-value or social exchange-value, called a price, determined not merely by individual valuations, but by social forces.[1] A price is strictly speaking a ratio, but for convenience prices are expressed as the quantity of some generalised commodity (money) that exchanges for a unit of the commodity under consideration. A good when brought to a market for purposes of exchange becomes a commodity. As we spoke of goods of the first, second, etc., orders, so, when these goods are offered for sale, we can call them commodities of the first, second, etc., orders. Cost-goods, when produced for the market, become cost-commodities. Goods subject to joint and composite demand become commodities subject to joint and composite demand. We thus get all kinds of commodities brought to market to be exchanged and brought away from the market, ultimately to be consumed. It is the characteristic of a perfect market that at any given time there is one and the same price for every portion of the stock of a commodity. Another character usually assumed to be present is that the quantity of a commodity on the market at a time is not small and that it is brought thither fairly regularly. Thus it is possible for there to exist some relation between the quantity being exchanged and the price at which exchange takes place. In the mathematical theory of price a continuous flow of commodities through the market is assumed.

19. Suppose there are a large number of persons desiring to buy a certain commodity: each will attribute to it a subjective exchange-value, an upper limit, more than which it is not worth while for him to offer for the commodity; this is his subjective demand-price. Similarly,

---

[1] There are two kinds of social forces that affect individual valuations. There is (a) the direct influence of social conventions on the individual consumer, as exemplified in the demand for top-hats and aspidistras, bibles and cocktail-shakers. Then there is (b) the fact that every social system involves a certain scheme of distribution of income, which distorts each individual's scale of valuation.

suppose a number of persons offering the same commodity for sale: each will have a lower limit for less than which he will not sell, but will consider it worth his while to retain the article or to put it to some alternative use; this is his subjective supply-price. Exchanging may start at any price at which there are both buyers and sellers. Of the persons desirous of buying, some, whose subjective demand-price is higher than the actual price, would continue buying whether the actual price rose or fell; others, whose subjective demand-price is just equal to the actual price, are the marginal buyers and would drop out if the price rose; the rest, whose subjective demand-price is less than the actual price, are excluded from buying and their demand only becomes effective if the latter falls below their demand-price. Thus the higher the actual price, the fewer effective buyers there are. Similarly, some would-be sellers are selling above their subjective supply-price; others, the marginal sellers, are selling at this price; the rest are excluded from selling. The higher the actual price, the more effective sellers there are. Whatever price exchange starts at it will not remain steady unless the quantity of the commodity offered to sellers at this price is equal to the quantity demanded at this same price by buyers. If the first price is too high, all the effective buyers will be satisfied, and there will still be left would-be sellers; therefore the price will have to fall till more buyers become effective. If the first price is too low, there will be an excess of buyers; therefore price will have to rise. At the price at which there are equal quantities of commodities demanded by persons willing to buy and offered by persons willing to sell, exchange can continue indefinitely. There can then be a permanent market with a flow of commodities into and out of it. This price is the normal market-price and is called the objective exchange-value of the commodity. (The term 'social exchange-value' might be preferable.) It is at the same time its objective demand-price and its objective supply-price. The movements of market-price are immediately controlled by the decisions of marginal buyers and sellers: the extent of its movements is determined by the subjective valuations of all the exchangers, effective and potential, who, however, unless they be for the moment marginal, have no influence in initiating the change. The objective exchange value of a commodity depends on the quantity changing hands in the market. What the relation between them is will be considered later. Here it must be emphasised that an objective exchange value is a quantity with two dimensions: it is not a mere money-equivalent but a money-equivalent and a quantity. The one is really meaningless without the other.

What is hereinafter referred to as market-price or normal market-price is an average of actual day-to-day quotations over a period of time sufficiently long to smooth out short-period fluctuations. The same refers to objective demand-price and to objective supply-price. For instance, a manufacturer may sell for a time below cost, but if he cannot cover his costs on the average over a period of time he will soon cease selling at all. A price always has reference to a regular flow through a market.

20. For any given quantity of the commodity passing through the market there is a price that will dispose of the whole supply; this depends on the buyers' subjective valuation, that is, in fact, the marginal buyer's subjective exchange-value (or subjective demand-price), but it is determined by social forces beyond any one individual's control and is thus an objective demand-price. Corresponding to any given quantity there is a determinate objective demand-price. A list of quantities with the corresponding demand-prices is called a demand-schedule. Expressed as a graph it is called a demand-curve.

21. As increased quantities of a commodity are put on a market the price that will carry off the whole supply falls. This for two reasons: Firstly, in accordance with the law of diminishing marginal utility, existing consumers will only purchase more at a low price. Secondly, would-be consumers that were below the margin of purchase, either because the commodity had a low use-value for them or because their resources were small, will be tempted by a lower price to enter the market. Thus Objective Demand-Price follows the same law as Subjective Use-Value: Value per unit diminishes with increasing quantity. This is the general law of demand in a market. As we shall see later (section 30) the same law applies to the demand for a commodity of order higher than the first.

22. While the value per unit always diminishes as the quantity increases, the aggregate value may either increase or diminish, according to the nature of the demand for the commodity. If purchasers are eager, a small increase in the quantity coming into the market may depress price by an amount so small that the total price paid for the whole supply, increases. If purchasers are easily satisfied, an increase of the quantity on offer will lower price by a more than proportionate amount, so diminishing the aggregate value. Thus we may classify demand as elastic or inelastic according as an increase in quantity offered increases or diminishes the aggregate value of the supply.[1]

---

[1] It can be easily shown that this is in accordance with Marshall's definition of elasticity of demand. For, if x denote quantity, y price per unit and z aggregate price, then $z = xy$ and $\dfrac{dz}{z} = \dfrac{dx}{x} + \dfrac{dy}{y}$. If e denote the Marshallian elasticity, then—

$$\frac{1}{e} = -\frac{dy}{y} \div \frac{dx}{x} = \left\{\frac{dx}{x} - \frac{dz}{z}\right\} \div \frac{dx}{x} = 1 - \frac{x}{z} \cdot \frac{dz}{dx}$$

Therefore, $e < = > 1$ according as $\dfrac{dz}{dx} < = > 0$.

23. Similarly, there is a price which will cause any given quantity of a commodity to be put upon the market; this is an objective supply-price and hence we obtain a supply-schedule and a supply-curve. The market price can then be considered as the price corresponding to the quantity at which supply-price and demand-price are equal; graphically it is said to be determined at the point of intersection of the supply-curve and the demand-curve. A modification is required in the above theory when production is carried on, as it is in the case of nearly all commodities under modern industrial civilisation, exclusively for the market. There is then no subjective supply-price and consequently we cannot derive objective supply-price from it.[1] Another quantity, to wit cost-price, becomes decisive in this case, but its consideration must be deferred for a while (sections 31–32). But in any case the objective demand-price still remains, and objective exchange-value is always identical with the demand-price of the quantity actually passing through the market.

24. We have now established a close parallel between subjective use-value and objective exchange-value. What the former is to the individual, the latter is to the society considered as an economic body. The whole theory of imputed value, of joint and composite demand and of costs can be paralleled with the substitution of objective for subjective value. In future the word value will be used, unless otherwise qualified, to denote the objective exchange-value or market-price. Two points must be noted, however. The first is that the objection to the theory of subjective value on the grounds of psychological over-simplification loses much of its validity, since it is

[1] Subjective supply-price exists in the case of the market for second-hand goods.

not every consumer or producer but the marginal ones whose judgments effect price changes. Now the existence in any community of even a few persons whose private economy is rational is sufficient to ensure a considerable degree of rationality in the economic activities of society as a whole. Thus the foundations of our theoretical edifice are really stronger than they may have seemed at first. We can proceed with the analysis of price determination in cases of joint demand or of joint supply in an industrial society with more security than we can with the analogous cases in the individual mind.

25. The second point is that while subjective exchange-value is derived directly from subjective use-value, we cannot reverse the process and assume the existence of a social or objective use-value from which objective exchange-value (demand-price) is derived. It is true that Wieser speaks of 'marginal equivalence', but this is an abstract conception derived from an exchange-economy, and does not express social marginal utility. Utility is essentially a subjective and individual thing. We cannot even compare directly two different individuals' utilities, but only infer a relation between them from the efforts they are prepared to make to obtain utilities. But the balancing of supply and demand in the market compares the quantities of resources people are prepared to offer in order to obtain various goods. Now, as we have seen, this depends partly on the intensity of their desire for the marginal unit of the good and partly on their own income. Now, in a community of persons with approximately equal incomes, a comparison of money offers would be a comparison of marginal utilities. The marginal buyer could then be considered as a kind of average member of society, and the marginal utility of the good to him could be taken as its social use-value, or marginal equivalence.[1] One could then infer an objective utility from the demand-schedule, and the analogy with individual valuation would be complete. But in a society of great inequalities this does not hold good. At the present time there is a shortage of working-class houses—it does not pay to build them—yet numbers of middle-class houses are being built. No one would suggest that the social need of working-class dwellings is less than that of dwellings for people who, on the average, are already more adequately housed than the working classes. Of a similar order is the paradox of bakers and bootmakers going unemployed while they and their families are hungry and ill-shod; in fact, all the ghastly contrast of luxury and waste side by side with poverty and want.

The analysis of price formation given here appears unduly fine-spun and prolonged; Marshall, who did much to introduce the theories of the Austrian School into Britain, condensed it considerably. But it is just the thing that he slurred over that is the most important point in it. In the transition from subjective use-value to subjective exchange-value is introduced the factor of marginal

---

[1] F. von Wieser, 'The Austrian School and the Theory of Value', *Economic Journal*, I, p. 108. 'Exchange-value and price follow the law of margins like value in use, with this qualification, they are determined directly, not by marginal utility, but by *marginal equivalence*, in which, not only supply and demand, but also the wealth of the purchaser is taken into account. . . . Prices cannot be taken without qualification as the social expression of the valuation of commodities; they are the result of a conflict waged over those commodities, in which power besides need, and more than need, has decided the issue. . . . Those misshapen prices which are engendered by monopolies, and those which, especially in the matter of wages, arise from the distress in the position of the labourer may be removed by a general coalition of labourers; but those which result from inequality in the means of purchasers are, I take it, inextricably bound up with our economic régime.'

Note also Taussig's concept of 'marginal vendibility' in his *Principles of Economics*, Ch. 9, § 4.

utility of income. The movements of price in an open
market are only a guide to social utility in a society substantially equalitarian. This was recognised by later
writers: Pigou's *Wealth and Welfare* and *Economics of
Welfare* devote a great deal of space to the consequences
of this fact. The social advantages of freely disposable
purchasing power and of the open market are offset by
the distortion that inequality of income introduces into
the measure of social utility. It cannot be too strongly
emphasised that the point at which this deflection first
appears in our analysis of price determination is in the
formation of a measure of exchange-value out of a purely
private and individual estimation of value. Nevertheless,
however the objective demand schedule of a commodity be
composed and although it can never coincide with any
individual's schedule of subjective demand-prices, it will
have the same property as an individual's subjective
demand schedule: the more of a commodity is offered, the
less value will it have.

26. The process of valuing successive increments and of
balancing alternative uses, described under subjective
value, goes on in the case of commodity production, only
here it is objective demand-price and not marginal utility
that is the criterion. Moreover, the process has become a
specialised function performed by a class of persons—
entrepreneurs—who do it for gain. Acting under the
stimulus of innumerable shifting objective prices of goods,
they determine the total quantity of goods to be produced,
they combine the various commodities of higher order
entering into the final product, including both material
goods and personal services, they adjust the proportions
in which these goods are combined, and they substitute
one constituent for another. The manner of supply of this
function, whether by an individual and if so, how chosen,

or by a corporation, private or public, and of its organisation and control, is not relevant here. Also, for simplicity's
sake, it will be assumed that it has no cost—that the entrepreneur does not absorb any of the price paid for the
finished commodity. (Later, in Chapter IV, sections 11,
23–26, 28, the cost of the entrepreneur's own services will
be considered.)

27. The demand for higher-order commodities is derived
from that of first-order commodities. Where a commodity
of higher order passes simply and solely into one of lower
order, the whole value of the latter is imputed to the
former. Where a commodity of higher order may pass
alternatively into several ones of lower order, a value is
imputed to it from each of the alternative lower-order
commodities. This is a case of composite demand. Where
a collection of higher-order commodities passes collectively
into a single one of lower-order, the whole value of the
latter is imputed to the group. This is a case of joint
demand.

28. In the case of composite demand a commodity has a
certain value imputed to it from each of its uses, the
lowest one being *the* value, but the operation of price and
of rational business organisation tends, by withdrawing it
from low-valued uses and directing it to high-valued uses,
to equalise its value in all uses. Two cases occur, according
as the commodity can be allotted in all proportions (within
limits) to its different uses or as natural and technical
conditions fix a definite proportion between them. An
example of the first case is wood, which can be used
(among other things) either for burning or for building
houses; and of the second case is cotton, yielding in a
definite and fixed proportion the joint products cotton-
wool (used for making cotton thread and hence cloth) and

cotton-seed (used for extracting oil). In the first case, the quantity devoted to each use can be adjusted separately; in the second case the quantity consumed of the commodity must be adjusted as a whole.

29. In the case of joint demand, where a commodity is produced by the combination of a group of several different constituents, the value of the whole group is derived from and equal to that of their product, but the attribution to each constituent of its proper share in the value of the whole is an intricate matter. An example of this is iron, the manufacture of which requires the use of iron-ore, coke and limestone in definite proportions. We know that iron-ore derives its value from the iron that it helps to make, but how much of the value of the iron is to be attributed to the ore and how much to the coke and to the limestone? Two main cases arise: (i) the constituents are combined in fixed proportions; (ii) the constituents are combined in proportions that can be varied, within limits, to give the same or a similar product.

In case (i) of fixed proportions, the possibility of separate valuation depends on the existence of alternative uses, outside the combination under consideration, for the various constituents. (That is to say on the co-existence of Composite along with Joint Demand.) This alternative use may be as a constituent in some other combination or it may be for the direct satisfaction of a consumer's want (i.e. as a commodity of the first order). If no constituent has any other use but in combination, then each of them is entirely useless without the others, and the problem of allocating to each constituent of the combination a definite share in the total value of the product becomes indeterminate. If some of the constituents have an alternative use then there are two ways in which a value can be imputed to one constituent. The first is directly, by the value imputed to it from that alternative use. The second is by residual value. Its residual value arises from the fact that if one constituent be taken from the combination the remaining constituents can no longer be used to produce the lower-order good; their value is therefore reduced from that of the lower-order good to the sum of the values of the remaining constituents considered separately. The difference between these values is the residual value of the good removed. This method is applicable to the valuation of one constituent when all the other constituents have each an alternative use. Then the value of one is equal to the value of the whole group diminished by the sum of the values in alternative employment of the others. This can be applied where one constituent only has no alternative use. Where more than one constituent is useless outside that particular combination, the constituents without alternative use can have a value attributed to them as a group, but it is impossible to apportion this value between them.

In the case (ii) of variable proportion we have at our disposal, in addition to the two methods of valuation already mentioned, a third. The third method is the method of marginal net products: it can be used where the proportions in which the constituents are combined can be slightly varied. The principle of this method is essentially a modification of that of residual value. Let the proportions in which the constituents are combined be varied slightly; so that instead of n units of one constituent $(n + 1)$ units are used, in conjunction with an unchanged quantity of the other constituents. Then the difference between the value of the product in the first case and that of the product in the second case is the value of the additional net product due to the use of one unit of the constituent in question. This will in general vary according to the initial proportions, but if the starting point be the technically most efficient combination of constituents for a given rate of output of the product, the contribution made by each constituent, estimated in this way, will be the marginal contribution of that constituent. This may be called the value of that constituent.

Where the value of goods in joint demand can be obtained by different methods the lowest is *the* value, but the operation of the market and of the entrepreneur tends so to allocate goods to different uses as to equalise all these values at the margin. If no constituent of the product has any value apart from its use in that combination and if no variation in proportions is possible, then the problem of valuation is insoluble.

30. The law of diminishing Demand-price holds good for higher-order commodities as well as for first-order commodities. In the case of simple demand this follows directly from diminishing Demand-price of the lower-order good into which a higher-order good is transformed—ultimately from the diminishing Demand-price of a consumption good. In the case of joint demand, each of the higher-order goods that jointly enter into a lower-order good has a diminishing Demand-price for two reasons: (a) the diminishing Demand-price of the product: (b) the fact that if one constituent is increased in quantity, the others remaining constant, a point of maximum technical efficiency is reached, after which its physical yield increases less than proportionately to the increased supply of constituent (law of Diminishing Returns). In the other complex cases of demand, the validity of the law of diminishing Demand-price is obvious.

31. Surveying the economic field as a whole, it is seen that by far the greatest majority of actual commodities are produced under conditions of both composite and joint

demand. Put in another way, there are a great number of
commodities belonging to higher orders that are combined
with one another in order to produce a great variety of
finished goods. Such are the constructional materials—
iron, wood, etc., textiles, sources of power, especially coal,
fluid capital ('credit') and human labour-power (especially
the less skilled kinds). These protean commodities are
cost-commodities: the value of a cost-commodity is a cost.
(objective or social cost: compare section 10, p. 72).
These, being goods in joint demand and being combined
in varying proportions, have imputed to them *a* marginal
net product in each of their uses. Competition will equalise
these marginal net products so that we may speak of *the*
marginal net product of a given cost-commodity. This is
its value. If, in any fresh combination of cost-commodities to form a new product, the sum of the values of the
constituents exceeds the value of the product, then the
proposed combination is uneconomic: the product is not
worth producing in that particular way, since it uses up
cost-goods that would engender more value in other uses.
If the sum of the values of the constituents is less than
the value of the product, a surplus will be realised, which,
under free competition, will be wiped out by increasing the output of the product and consequently lowering
its value. (If one of the constituents of the product is
not a cost-good, a residual value will be imputed to it.)
Thus the sum of the values of the cost-constituents of a
product—shortly called the cost of the product—becomes
a touchstone of the economic worth-whileness of the
branch of production in question. The values of most cost
goods being comparatively stable and known, the entrepreneur carries on production by their guidance. Hence
arises the general opinion that costs determine value. In
truth, they are themselves determined ultimately by demand. In short, cost-commodities receive their value by

the process of imputation from their marginal use and then pass this value back to all their other uses by a reverse process, which we may call deputation. This deputed value, that is, value that a good of lower order derives from goods of a higher order entering into its composition, corresponds to the ordinary idea of a cost.

Costs are obviously analogous with the opportunity-costs of individual economy. In fact, disutility-costs scarcely enter at all into developed capitalist economy. Opportunity-cost thus appears to be synonymous with the value of a production-good that is in both composite and joint demand.

32. Having developed the theory of objective costs we can now proceed to that of objective supply-price. In a capitalistic economy the objective supply-price, i.e. the price which will tempt a given quantity of a commodity into the market, depends on cost-price, i.e. the sum of the costs of its constituents. In any case cost-price forms a lower limit below which supply cannot permanently continue. Under conditions of free competition, rival entrepreneurs undercut each other and force each other to the lower limit. Hence, if a commodity is freely reproducible it will be multiplied until its value has sunk to its cost and in this case supply-price becomes identical with cost-price. Under a sellers' monopoly the value can be raised above cost, the difference being called net monopoly revenue, which is thus a function both of cost and of demand. A private monopoly tends to make this a maximum; a public monopoly can choose whether to draw an income from this source, to sell at cost (thus reproducing in this respect the conditions of free competition) or even to sell below cost and recoup itself from some other source.

Thus, given information as to the technical and institutional conditions of production of the commodity, we can construct a supply-schedule, connecting quantity with supply-price. Objective demand-price and objective supply-price stand opposite each other, just as their subjective analogies did. But it must not be forgotten that this parallelism is only formal. All supply-prices are derived ultimately from demand-prices. There is no real dualism in the theory of value.[1]

33. When value and cost coincide, then resources are being pushed into different uses in every direction, so as to yield the same marginal returns. This has two consequences. One is that the value of every commodity is as low as possible consistent with the rival claims of other branches of production, that therefore the quantities consumed are the greatest possible and that therefore there is the maximum satisfaction of wants. The second is that, since any transference of resources from one use to another would lower their marginal net product in the second use below the general level, the lowering of value to cost ensures the optimum use of resources. Under these circumstances, therefore, we get the apportionment of resources so as to yield the greatest satisfaction that they are capable of affording, within the limits of the price system and of inequality of income.

34. As stated above, the value of a good tends to equal its cost. If, however, the production of a good is limited, either by natural or artificial causes, its value will not fall to its cost: there will remain a surplus of value over cost. In the particular case of a good the quantity of which is unalterable by man's economic activity, the concept of

[1] See F. von Wieser, *Natural Value*, Bk. V, ch. vi; H. J. Davenport, *Economics of Enterprise*, ch. viii; P. Wicksteed, *Common Sense of Political Economy*, Bk. I., ch. ix.

cost has no place. Such a good has no supply price: its value is determined entirely by demand. Land is a typical case: the return to land is determined entirely by demand. In this case the return is called rent; hence we may speak of the rent element in the value of such goods. This difference is not, however, an absolute one; there are gradations in the natural restrictions of supply, from the original and indestructible properties of the soil down to goods that are totally and instantaneously destroyed in the process of use.

Note that fixity of supply is not necessary for the rent principle to operate: what is necessary is independence of supply. For instance, in a volcanic archipelago, islands might emerge from the sea and disappear again in such a manner as to produce a very variable supply of land: nevertheless, since the supply is not affected by the price received for it, the value of such land is still subject to the rent principle.

The element of time is an important one: a good may be freely reproducible, but during the time that must elapse before the stock of old ones can be replaced by new, the return on the old ones partakes of the nature of rent. In the case of goods that are impermanent and that have a supply-price, the cost at once affects the supply and by shifting the margin brings the average value of the return into equality with the discounted value of the cost (for explanation of discount, see *infra*, Chapter IV, section 16). There is an intermediate class of goods that have a supply price but are so durable that their cost of production has no immediate effect upon their supply and hence upon their return. In the long run these conform to the same law of equality of costs with average returns as the first class, but for any particular short period their return is of the nature of rent, and is denoted a quasi-rent.[1]

[1] A. Marshall, *Principles of Economics*, V, viii, 6.

Goods which are reproducible, but whose supply is limited by artificial means, have a definite cost, which may be called their supply-price, but they are not, in fact, offered for sale at that price. Owing to the limitation of supply, demand price (and, in consequence, actual selling price) is permanently above cost-price. Goods can therefore be divided into two classes (Wieser's cost-goods and monopoly-goods) which the writer proposes to term unrestricted goods and restricted goods.

Restriction must be distinguished from scarcity. Everything valuable is naturally scarce, but is not for that reason restricted. Scarcity is the condition for the emergence of value. Restriction is the condition for an emergence of an excess of value over cost. Restriction must also be distinguished from ordinary commercial monopoly, which is a special case of it. Although the word monopoly is often used in the wider sense, as when the private ownership of land is spoken of as a monopoly, or as in Wieser's use of the term monopoly-goods, it seems best to use it in the more limited sense and to coin a new term, Restriction, for the more extended signification.[1]

35. We must now study the effect of Restriction upon price formation in a market-economy. In the absence of Restriction cost-price becomes equal to demand-price and hence to market-price; just as scarcity is reflected in price, so is Restriction reflected in a selling-price higher than cost-price. Three kinds of Restriction are important.

[1] Oppenheimer uses the term '*Monopol*' in the sense of our 'Restriction'. Monopoly in the narrow sense he designates '*Tausch-monopol*', while the term '*Klassenmonopol*' corresponds to our 'Institutional Restriction'. He says 'Monopoly (*Monopol*) can also exist when several producers, not united by common agreement into a single economic collective person, share a position of power, while competing among one another', i.e. form a non-competing group, in Cairnes's phrase. (F. Oppenheimer, *Grundriss der theoretischen Ökonomik*, 1910, § **33**, 2.)

The first arises through natural irreproducibility, as in the case of land and natural products. These commodities have no supply-price and their value is derived entirely from their return. The second is ordinary monopoly, where one seller or a combination of such controls enough of the supply as to be able to fix the price in his own interest, with the effect of restricting output below what it would be if production were pushed to the margin in every direction (i.e. as in ideal free competition). The third arises through the action of social institutions, embodied in law, custom, and tradition. (Strictly speaking ordinary monopoly is a special case of this third kind.) This it is proposed to term Institutional Restriction, and it will be fully discussed in the chapter on Personal Distribution.

We thus see that any form of Restriction produces a surplus. In the case of natural Restriction this surplus is of the nature of rent and the value of the use of the restricted commodity is said to be determined on the rent-principle. In the case of Restriction due to social institutions a surplus also emerges and the investigation of this surplus and its ultimate incidence is an important but neglected part of the theory of distribution.

CHAPTER IV

THEORY OF FACTOR-DISTRIBUTION

1. It will be noticed that into the enumeration of cost-goods entered some things, such as capital and labour-power, that are usually included among the factors of production. Now every element entering into the selling price of a commodity can ultimately be analysed into payments made to persons for doing something or for refraining from doing something. These services are the factors of production: they are the goods of highest order. Combined in almost infinite variety to produce all the commodities on the market they are pre-eminently subject to composite and joint demand. They are the ultimate cost-goods. Society, in so far as its institutions embody the principle of economic rationality, organises the production process with the object of producing the greatest output at the least cost. Hence it treats the factors of production as cost-goods to be combined, balanced, and mutually substituted at the margin of production in such a way as to maximise the total net return. Since factors are capable of substitution for one another within a wide range of possible proportions in order to realise the same result, the method by which they are most usually valued is that of marginal net products. To the person who supplies a factor of production, its value is his income; hence we say that the return to every factor is its marginal net product. In this way a theory that from one aspect offers an explanation of the valuation of cost-goods becomes, when viewed from another aspect, a theory that explains the income accruing to the owners of certain factors of production.

2. We have spoken of the factors of production in a general way, without considering any particular factors. It is necessary to attempt some enumeration and classification. Both the traditional trio of land, labour, and capital and the modern quartette of land, labour, capital and organisation are unsatisfactory from many points of view. Factors of production are neither so few nor so uniform. Land for instance is demanded independently for different purposes while the supply is adapted to different uses and cannot be substituted in all cases for every other. Labour is of many kinds, each of which has its own conditions of supply and of demand. Truer would it be to say that the factors of production, like the commodities in which they are ultimately embodied, are legion; that there are innumerable grades and kinds of land, labour, instrumental goods, etc., co-operating in the production process and all forming independent factors of production. When this diversity is recognised, however, there is some convenience in classifying them under certain main heads. The Old Three are perhaps more suitable than the New Four.

3. The first broad distinction is between Man and Nature: all production of goods is the result of the activity of a certain organism—man—in his physical environment; to the goods produced both the activity and the environment have contributed. Hence the widest division is into the natural objects given by nature to the economic animal to work with—technically called Land—and the activity of the economic animal himself. Such activity includes not only the planning and the carrying out of work of all sorts—physical and mental—but also the provision and use of instrumental goods. These goods represent an application of human effort to the natural environment directed so as to produce not immediate gratifications but the material potentiality of future gratifications. They

owe their existence to man's effort, but once they have come into being they resemble natural objects in many respects. They form part of the passive environment on which man acts to produce wealth. In fact, in the case of many durable instruments of production, it becomes impossible in time to distinguish between the natural and the artificial. This suggests a different line of division— not between Man and Nature, but between Work and Instruments, including only actual labour and organisation in the first, and lumping together in the second, all passive instruments of production, whether immediately given by nature or produced by antecedent labour on materials originally given by nature. (This corresponds to Dr. Cannan's division between Work and Property.)

Practical convenience, therefore, dictates a threefold division: the familiar trinity of Labour, Capital and Land. Under Capital will be included not only the provision of instrumental goods, but also the productive use of them, that is to say, the factors of production now usually distinguished under the titles, Waiting (Saving, or Capital in the narrow sense of the factor whose return is pure Interest) and Uncertainty-bearing (Risk-taking or Enterprise, the factor whose return is pure Profit).

The classification of factors of production at which we have arrived is given in the table on p. 101.

Including the division of Capital into two, the main groups of factors of production, with the names that are here given to their returns, are as follows:—

I. Labour		Wages
II. Capital	1. Waiting	Interest
	2. Uncertainty-bearing	Profit
III. Land		Rent

These must be understood as complex categories, covering, as in the case of Land and Labour, many qualitative kinds and many quantitative grades. More-over, under Labour will be discussed various kinds of Organisation, appearing under widely different forms in different social systems. Only the factor of Waiting can be considered as a single uniform factor of production. All the others are mere classificatory divisions into which are sorted the real factors of production, which, it should

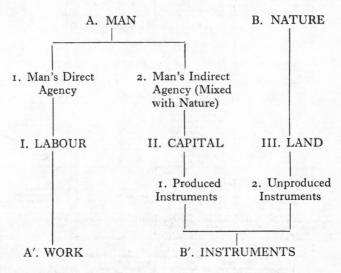

be repeated, are as many and as various as the ultimate goods themselves.

This classification is unsatisfactory from many points of view. For instance, it separates Land from the two categories into which Capital has been resolved. Now from the individual point of view property in the soil does not differ from property in buildings or machinery: the acquisition of both alike involves waiting. Under the existing social system, land becomes merged with other factors, in the general category of Property, as opposed to work: an antithesis that is important both from the individual and from the social point of view. On the whole, however, the fact that no Waiting is entailed on society as a whole in the provision of Land, however much individuals may have to save in order to acquire previously appropriated pieces of land, makes the distinction between it and other forms of property valuable from the social point of view.

Again, the choice of discriminating terms between Labour and Organisation on the one hand and Waiting and Uncertainty-bearing on the other is a difficult one. I have used the words 'direct' and 'indirect' respectively, since in one case the human agent performs directly some act or series of acts and in the other he merely allows instrumental goods in his control to be devoted to certain uses.

4.   I. LABOUR

Labour may be defined as any sort of personal activity of economic significance. The return to Labour is Wages. The term is used in economics in an extended sense, to include not only a payment made under a contract of service by an employer to an employee but any earnings of an individual's personal activities, whether obtained through contract with an entrepreneur, through direct bargaining with the consumer of the goods produced, or through payment in any way by a public authority. It thus includes wages (usually so-called), salaries, fees, commission, and the earnings of a man working on his own account (after deduction of Rent and Interest, if any).

5. The factors included under the term Labour may be classified in two ways: first, horizontally, according to the kind of product made or service rendered, i.e. by industry and trade; and second, vertically, according to the grade of skill or responsibility. According to the latter basis of division four grades may be recognised:

unskilled manual labour; skilled manual labour and mental labour involving no responsibility; responsible and/or specialised mental labour (managerial, technical and professional work); creative labour in science, art, government, or the direction of industry.

6. The demand for any kind of labour is derived from the productivity of such labour: to be precise from the value of the extra product of an extra unit (the marginal net product) of the factor. This law is true, in general, whatever be the institutional forms under which Labour is exerted. In slave economy, in serf economy, in wage-labour economy, or in free-labour economy the marginal net product indicates the rate above which the work will not, in the long run, be remunerated.[1] This appears most clearly under conditions of wage-labour, where the entrepreneur consciously hires and fires labour on the principle that he will not employ men unless it pays him to do so; but a slave-owner will not give his slaves more than they are worth in the way of food, shelter, etc. (their income under the system), and a free labourer is employed by the general public (as, indeed, is the wage labourer, through the mediation of the professional entrepreneur) from whom he cannot in the long run obtain more for his wares than their market value. Where wage labour and free labour co-exist, then the competition of free labourers with wage labourers employed by professional entrepreneurs is an additional force tending to bring the remuneration of free labour under the speedy and responsive operation of the law of marginal net products.

It is sometimes urged that collective bargaining has nullified the valuation of labour according to marginal

---

[1] Thus far most economists go: but can the work be remunerated below the rate? This point must be reserved till the next chapter (section 12).

net products. It is true that collective bargaining makes
more difficult certain kinds of adjustments. For instance,
the establishment of a standard day, with the condition
that a full day must be paid for even if the worker works
only for a few hours and that overtime must be paid for
all time in excess of the standard, forces the employer to
purchase the workers' time in blocks of a certain minimum
size. This means adjustment of the time to the nearest
day instead of to the nearest hour: at a given hourly rate
the number of hours bought will be determined by the
yield of an hour's work of the marginal day and will stop
short of the marginal hour, thus less labour will be hired
than if the finer adjustment to the marginal hour had
been possible. Similarly, if a group of so many men of
certain grades or of so many men of certain grades in
conjunction with a particular machine must be employed
as an indivisible unit, the marginal worker is not the
marginal individual but the man belonging to the marginal
group: at a given rate of wages slightly fewer men will
be employed. Nevertheless, provided employers (or in
the ultimate analysis the consuming public) are free to
choose how many workers will be employed under the
terms of a given collective bargain the determination of
the value of labour according to its marginal net product
still takes place.

The process is rendered more certain if it is possible
for substitution to take place. This is usually the substitution, not of one kind of labour for another, but of
one kind of labour in combination with one sort of instrument of production for another kind of labour in conjunction with another sort of instrument of production.
Even if it is difficult for such substitution to take place
in the production of a given commodity, it can frequently
take place through the substitution for one commodity
of another, involving the use of different kinds of labour.

Moreover, although the direct substitution of one kind of labour for another is often difficult to effect at once, it takes place readily over a period of years.

7. With respect to the supply of Labour some difficult points must be discussed. About the supply of Labour as a whole nothing definite can be predicated.[1] It is obviously not a fixed quantity, for it can be increased in three ways: first, by increase in the numbers of the employed population (either by growth in the numbers of those sex and age groups that are habitually employed or by an extension of habitual employment to sex and age groups not previously so engaged); second, by extending the working hours or days of those already at work; and third, by increasing the intensity or efficiency of labour during the hours of work. Only in the case of the third way is it possible to discover any such definite relation between the price offered (wages) and the quantity of labour forthcoming as can be made the basis of a supply schedule. In the case of the second way, although the offer of a higher rate may stimulate the supply of some hours of overtime, wages and normal hours of labour vary in opposite senses as often as in the same sense. In the case of the first way (changes in the number of the population) no definite relation can be traced between wages in general and numbers in general. The old conception of a rigid relation based on the tendency of wages to fall to subsistence level has no basis in facts. On the contrary, the available evidence seems to show that in all ages and climes the 'brazen law of wages' is the expression of abnormal and transitory phenomena rather than of a normal trend. The attempt to preserve the law formally by the substitution of a customary standard of life for

[1] See D. H. Robertson, 'Economic Incentive', *Economica*, No. 3, October, 1921.

subsistence reduces the whole contention to an argument
in a circle, for the standard of life depends on the wages
that can be got. The fact seems to be that the supply of
Labour as a whole is governed by a set of causes, as yet
very imperfectly known, that have no obvious relation
to Wages as a whole. Thus the return to Labour, like that
to Land, is governed by the rent principle. What the
workers collectively get is determined not directly by their
own exertions but by the social demand for their products.
The demand for Labour is derived from its marginal net
product, which is determined at least as much by the
efficiency and by the conditions of supply of other factors
as by the efficiency of Labour. It is also affected by the
scale of output of the product.

8. This view must be modified when we come to consider
the various concrete kinds of labour that are grouped
under the general designation Labour. The supply of
labour to a particular trade may be augmented by the
flow of workmen into it out of other trades, if the wages
that can be got in it are higher than those prevailing for
labour of similar quality in other trades. The total supply
of labour is unaltered, but its allocation to particular uses
is affected, as in the case of land. Within the limits of one
trade or grade an increase of wages may call forth an
extra supply of exertion, either in duration, intensity, or
efficiency. In these cases the supply of labour to particular
trades and grades will have, in general, a functional relation
to the additional remuneration. Given a normal level of
wages, determined as above on the rent principle, there
will be a supply schedule relating wage-differentials to
the supply of any particular kind of labour. This is especially marked in the case of the more specialised, skilled
or responsible kinds of labour (i.e. the second and third
of the four grades enumerated in section 5). Although

the supply of the lowest grade of labour is indeterminate, that of skilled or directive labour is fairly closely related on the one hand to the extra inducements held out to other workers to engage upon it, and on the other hand to the expenses and efforts which these workers must make to qualify themselves for it. Thus we can speak of a supply-price for this kind of labour. When we come to the fourth kind of labour—creative work—we again find that the conditions of supply are indeterminate, partly because the rarity of such cases and the individual character of each tend to withdraw it from the sphere of economic generalisation, but mainly because it is exerted in obedience to a psychological necessity of its possessor: he would do that kind of work irrespective of his reward simply because he has it in him to do it. The whole return to labour of this sort is, therefore, subject to the rent-principle.

9. Certain kinds of human activity give rise to special problems in the theory of factor-distribution. They are those connected with social organisation.

In economic society there are institutions which, whether they are themselves immediately concerned with the production of wealth or not, help to maintain and direct the economic life of society. The institutions that we are particularly concerned with are those of Labour Organisation, the Organisation of Enterprise, and Government. The persons who staff the organisations in which these institutions are embodied do not concern themselves so much with any particular piece of work or unit of output as with the initiation and conditions of production, and with the relations between particular pieces of work or units of output. This activity of initiation and co-ordination is essentially a kind of Labour; but it is so closely connected with the working of social institutions, it is necessarily collective and social to such an extent, and some aspects of it are so specialised and subject to peculiar conditions, that it requires special theoretical treatment.

In the case of all three forms of organisation it is the activities of persons that is being discussed, but by a figure of speech these can be referred to under the title of the institutions which they serve. Thus one can speak of the cost of a Trade-Union and the marginal net product of a State Department when one really means the cost of the activities of the persons running the Union or the marginal net product of officials of the Department.

In some cases the persons who provide these activities enjoy no specially privileged opportunities compared with other workers: they are either salaried servants of a public corporation, salaried servants of a private corporation, or free-lances operating under competitive conditions. An example of the first is any civil servant; examples of the second are a trade-union official, or the director of a joint-stock company; the independent business man in a non-monopolised trade is an example of the third. Such persons are really labourers, even though of a specialised kind, their earnings are governed by the same influences as those of other labourers of similar qualifications.

The connection of these workers with the institutional framework, however, gives them special opportunities for creating monopoly conditions and acquiring additional income thereby. Thus the private organiser of industry may agree with his fellows to restrict output and so raise profits above what competition would determine. In some countries trade-union officials make their position a source of income over and above the salary voted them by their constituents, by accepting money from employers for making settlements on terms favourable to the latter or by accepting money from some employers for calling strikes in their rivals' establishments. Again the functions of government were performed under the feudal system by owners of lordships that conferred large and indefinite incomes of sovereignty on their holders, and even under the bourgeois-democratic régime a seat in some legislative assemblies is a source of profit to its occupant through the opportunities it gives for accepting bribes from business interests or for speculation based on access to confidential sources of knowledge.

10. (a) *Labour Organisation.*—The function of Labour Organisation is analogous on the one hand to Enterprise (a co-operative workshop, for example, fulfils both functions) and on the other to Government. Its claim to rank as a factor of production rests on the same grounds as that of Government; it has a definite cost and a definite return, equal to the net marginal product of resources invested in it, although no special name has been given to this return. Like the earnings of Business Organisation, it may contain monopoly elements. When, however, labour organisations are strong enough to create a monopoly in their members' services, the revenue therefrom usually appears in the form of a monopoly element in these members' Wages rather than in the remuneration of the organisers themselves.

11. (b) *Organisation of Enterprise.*—The demand for the service of the business organiser is its net marginal product, determined partly, as in the case of free labour, by the competition of buyers for the commodities that the entrepreneur helps to produce (the public employs the entrepreneur and the entrepreneur employs the other factors of production), and partly, as in the case of wage labour, by the process of hiring and firing by other entrepreneurs,

since some at least of the functions of enterprise can be exercised by salaried persons in the employ of public or private corporations. This fact affects not only the salaried business organisers concerned, but also, through their actual or potential competition with independent entrepreneurs, all business organisers of whatever kind, as in the case of labour discussed above (p. 103).

The supply of business organisation depends, on the whole, upon the same influences as that of other kinds of work requiring ability and specialised training. That is to say it depends first of all on certain personal qualities and secondly on the social organisation that gives these qualities the opportunity of developing and the opportunity for their employment when developed. It is undoubted that business ability is a specialised and not very common kind of ability. It appears to differ from most other kinds of ability in that it can exist in and by itself, uncorrelated with ability in other activities of life outside its own sphere. This fact makes it very difficult to judge of the real frequency of its occurrence. It may be that it is as infrequent as the existing numbers of the class suggest, that all those who have it struggle somehow through the press and put it to use, and that changes in social conditions could do little towards mitigating its scarcity. We know that there are poets and philosophers in our elementary schools, only waiting for opportunity to unfold their talent: perhaps potential business geniuses make their own opportunities. On the other hand it may be that under different social conditions a greater supply of business ability could be obtained and at a lower social cost.

The institutions that seem to favour the development of organising ability are those comprised in the term Education, including not only formal apprenticeship and the set teaching of schools and colleges, but also the varied arrangements under which one may gain experience of men and affairs. Thus, as against the expansion of organised commercial education, must be set the departmentalising of large businesses, in which the junior employee, confined to a mechanical task, loses contact with actual management and enterprise. The institutions that give scope for enterprise are, first of all, political and economic freedom, the removal of legal or traditional barriers to rationalised and individualised economy. All forms, however, of the organisation of business and of capital tend to have an influence on the supply on this function. The joint-stock company, the fluidity and cheapness of credit, the organised and localised market, and the dissemination of accurate technical and commercial information all favour an increased supply of business ability at a given price.

12. *Business Monopoly.*—Monopoly, in the restricted commercial sense, must be discussed under the heading of enterprise, since the business organiser has unrivalled opportunities for exercising monopoly-power. At certain stages in the development of this function it becomes easier and more remunerative to organise for the purpose of controlling the output, and hence the market, than for that of supplying the public with what it demands. By reducing output below the point at which normal market equilibrium is established, a surplus of price over cost emerges. This surplus, multiplied by the number of units sold is the monopolists' net monopoly-revenue. The perfect monopolist will aim at the rate of output for which this quantity is a maximum. In practice this is rarely attained, partly because of insufficient knowledge of market conditions, and partly because few monopolies are absolute. Competition, actual or potential, nearly always exists, if not of other producers of the same com-

modity, at any rate of other commodities that may be substituted for the one monopolised. The existence of monopoly-price is often obscured by the economies effected through combination, but even if the selling-price after combination is less than before it contains, if the cost-price has been still more reduced, an element of monopoly-revenue. If, however, the only way in which the community can get its organising work done for it is by tolerating the formation of monopolies and their exactions, then such revenue must be reckoned as part of the normal earnings of the business organiser and hence as part of the necessary costs of production.

To establish monopoly it is necessary to control output. This can be done in either of two cases: one is when there is only one firm engaged in the trade, the other is when there is a combination of all the firms with a common policy regarding output and price. It is necessary, more-over, not only to control existing output, but to restrict the entry of new firms into the trade.

13. Two stages are theoretically possible in the development of monopoly-power in industry. In the first it is confined to particular trades or industries, in the second it is general. In the first stage, that of partial monopoly, entre-preneurs in each monopolised industry seek to maximise monopoly-revenue in that industry. To do this they restrict output and therefore drive factors of production out of that industry into non-monopolised industries. The result is a mal-distribution of productive resources, the marginal net product of each factor is lower than it would be under ideal competition; the total social product is reduced, but the monopolists acquire a greater absolute share.

The second stage, general monopoly, implies more than the establishment in every industry of a partial monopoly of the kind described above. The result of this would be a state of unstable equilibrium similar to that of duopoly, familiar in the mathematical theory of the subject.[1] General monopoly implies a monopolistic organisation of industry as a whole, regulating the output of each and every industry in order to maximise the income of the class that controls industry. The result would be a lower level of production and a lower marginal net product of non-monopolised factors of production, than under ideal competition, but factors of production would be allocated to the different branches of industry in the most advantageous manner for that level of production. While ideal competition would maximise the total social product and the marginal net product of every factor of production, general monopoly would maximise the absolute share of property owners.

In the present development of capitalist economy, monopoly is in the first stage, but there are hints of the emergence of the second stage. Rationalisation of industry, the consolidation of banking and finance, centralised control of new issues and rationing of the supply of credit to industry, control of money rates by central banks—all these are creating the possibility of general monopoly. To realise this potentiality all that is necessary is to change the object of control from the maximisation of production to the maximisation of profit. At present, for example, the organisation of the money market tends to force capital into every possible use and to lower the rate of interest. A little tightening of central control, however, could manipulate interest rates so as to maintain a slightly lower level of production and, at the cost of leaving some capital unemployed, force up aggregate profits at the expense of wages.

Imagine a community producing a single commodity: wheat, and composed of two classes: farmers (owning

[1] See A. L. Bowley, *Mathematical Groundwork of Economics*, ch. ii, §3.

land, capital and business opportunities) and labourers. Both farmers' profits and labourers' wages take the form of portions of wheat. Farmers and labourers can be treated as non-competing groups exchanging services of property and services of labour respectively, both kinds of services being priced in terms of wheat. Competition among farmers will push the production of wheat up to the point at which so much is produced as will sell at prices so low as to leave the marginal farmer no better off than a labourer. The total production of wheat will be the same as that of an ideal communistic society and the labourers' share will be as high as it could be without socialising the income of the supra-marginal farmers. But if farmers refrain from competing with one another, they can make the rate of interchange of services more favourable to themselves. Less wheat will be produced, but farmers will get more of it. Farmers will part with considerably less wheat, in order to obtain rather less labourers' services.

14. (c) *Government.*—Although not usually enumerated among the factors of production, the maintenance of the legal framework which enshrines the institutions of property and contract, of freedom and restriction, and within which the productive forces work, has as much claim to be regarded as a productive service and to have imputed to it a share in the value of the social joint-product as the organising and enterprising functions that set the productive forces in motion.[1] It is not only a productive service, but definite quantitative relations exist between

[1] Knies, Roscher and Wagner reckon the State as part of Capital. Roscher (*Lehrbuch*, I, § 42), enumerating different kinds of capital, says 'Immaterial Capital. The most important immaterial capital in every community is indeed the State itself.' For Wagner's views, see his *Grundlagen der Volkswirtschaftslehre*, Bk. III, ch. i, §§ 149-151, and the whole of his Book VI. See also G. Schmoller, *Grundriss der Volkswirtschaftslehre*, Einleitung, I, and also Book II, 3.

it and its return. Its cost is the cost of maintaining the system of government as measured in taxes, dues, local rates, loans, depreciation of the currency, the profits of public monopolies, requisitions, customary services, forced labour, etc., to all of which we shall apply the generalised term of Taxes. Its marginal net product is the addition to the value of the annual social product made by the expenditure of an additional unit of resources on governmental services. At any given stage of economic and political development there is a point in the extension of governmental activities at which the net product of the marginal government service is just equal to the gross burden of the marginal tax. At this point the economic benefit of government is a maximum: below this point an increased expenditure on government will more than pay for itself; above this point further taxation becomes an unproductive burden.

The nature of this factor is concealed, under modern conditions, by the fact that it is a public monopoly, provided by states and municipalities and that its return does not appear to enter into any individual's income. (Its immediate return forms the earnings of public servants, and is a form of the Wages of Labour, but it is referred to specially here for the reasons mentioned in section 9.) But in other periods this factor was privately organised and its return was an important constituent of some individuals' incomes. According to the theory of the Feudal System, land was held on condition that its holder provided many of those services of protection and jurisdiction that the State now performs. Thus the income of a feudal lord was analytically composed of two portions: the Rent of Land and the return on governmental functions. (This distinction was recognised in practice by the French National Assembly, which, on the famous night of August 4, 1789, while carefully preserving and guaranteeing property-rights, such as rent of land, and hire of buildings, abolished feudal rights, as such, without compensation.) The brigand chief, who levies an annual tax on the peaceful merchants and cultivators of his neighbourhood as the condition of his not molesting them and even of his protecting them from rival robbers, is providing the function of government and enjoying the fruits of his abstinence in Taxes. Until the community can so organise itself as to provide its own protection cheaper and better by co-operative action, so long must it pay tribute to the brigands in order to induce them not to exercise their destructive power, just as at present the community pays Interest to rich people in order to induce them to refrain from using their legal right of consuming wealth that ought to be used for further production. Not only has modern economics rehabilitated Ruskin's 'bag-baron', but it is able to place the 'crag-baron' beside his brother on the high pedestal dedicated to hard-working public servants.[1]

15. II. CAPITAL.

We now come to one of the thorniest and most discussed parts of the theory of factor-distribution: the nature of the return to capital, or to state it in the form in which it is usually put, the nature of interest.

It is not enough to point to the physical productivity of instrumental goods: physical production is not necessarily the production of values. If the value of a collection of goods of higher order is derived from the value of the collection of goods of lower order that result from them, why is not the whole value of the product imputed to the instrumental goods, raw materials, etc., entering into them? In other words, what causes the production of instrumental goods to fall short of the point at which

---

[1] J. Ruskin, *Crown of Wild Olive*, § 44.

interest would cease to exist? Some hitherto overlooked element in the process of valuation must exist to account for this. This element is introduced by the time-relations of production. These have two aspects, the physical and the psychological. There is first the physical fact that most processes of production involving the use of material instruments take time. As a general rule the more developed industry becomes the more it makes use of roundabout methods of production.[1] Instead of immediately making things that we want, we make things to make things that ultimately contribute towards making the things we want. A greater product is obtained, but there is an increase in the time elapsing between the initiation of the first processes in the chain of production and the production of the finished article. This lapse of time involves two things. First, it is necessary that those who initiated the earlier processes of production should wait for the final product. Second, there is introduced into production an element of uncertainty, because, during the time taken for the product to mature, the conditions that originally made its production seem worth while may change. In other words, capitalist production involves both waiting and uncertainty-bearing. Now we must take into consideration the psychological aspect. There is, first, the fact that people are unwilling to wait: that they have a preference for present goods over future ones. In other words there is a difference between the subjective values of two physically similar goods that are to be enjoyed at different times. There is, second, the fact that people are unwilling to expose their resources to uncertainty: that the subjective value of the future product is diminished by the risk that it may, after all, not be wanted. All these facts taken together, the fact that the most productive

[1] Term used by Smart to translate Böhm-Bawerk's 'Produktions-umwege'.

methods involve waiting and that the consumer discounts the value of future goods, the fact that the most productive methods involve risk and that this risk makes the productive use of resources less attractive, are responsible for the difference between the value of a product and the value of the goods that enter into it. Thus Capital resolves itself into the two functions of Waiting and Uncertainty-bearing.

16. (i) *Waiting.*—Three chief causes can be assigned to the preference for present goods over future ones. The first is the prospective undervaluation of future goods, due to the less vivid realisation of future needs. This undervaluation depends on the amount of income and is relatively greater the less the income of the person concerned. The second depends on what Fisher calls the time-shape of income and Böhm-Bawerk the relation between needs and provision for needs with different people at different times in their lives. When future income is greater than present income, the utility of equal resources will be less in the future than in the present and therefore time-preference will be higher than it would be as determined by the first cause alone. When future income is less than present, the utility of each unit of future resources will be greater. But, while future goods can only be enjoyed in the future, present goods can, in most cases, be kept for future use, and therefore only in the few cases where resources cannot be stored will time-preference become less than zero. Thus in some cases time-preference will be increased by this second cause; in many cases it will be unaffected; in only a few cases it will be diminished and very exceptionally may even become negative (i.e. future goods at an agio). The third cause is the uncertainty of income. If income is likely to be more variable in the distant future than in the near future, it will be worth while to make some provision for such a contingency and time-preference will be lowered. If the reverse holds good, provision for the near future will take precedence over that for remoter points of time and time-preference will be raised. Since diminution of need is equivalent to increase of provision or of income, the effect of the shortness and uncertainty in length of human life is to raise time-preference. Few people value a quantity of resources in the hands of a distant heir as highly as an equal quantity in their own. The general result of these three cases, which operate cumulatively, is to give most persons a very definite positive time-preference—i.e. they undervalue future goods. Moreover the smaller the income the greater the utility of present goods; thus the poorer the individual the higher as a rule, is his rate of discounting the future.

17. Collective bodies as well as individuals express a time-preference in their economic dealings. (Hence a socialistic community would have to take interest into account, not, however, as a form of payment to individuals, but as a measure of the worth-whileness of applying resources to ends not immediately productive.[1])

The collective time-preference of a group is determined by similar forces to those that govern individual time-preference. Other things being equal, a group of poor persons will have a higher time-preference than a group of rich persons. But the influence of factors other than that of need and provision for need tends to make collective time-preferences lower than individual ones. As soon as a group acquires a sense of communal personality the shortness and uncertainty of human life exerts a less powerful influence, hence a group of persons of a given income level may be expected to show more regard for

[1] See Appendix to Chapter IV, pp. 142–145.

the future in their collective transactions than as individuals (consider for instance the co-operative societies). Secondly, since a man does not miss what he has never had, he can be persuaded to forgo the use of a sum that is due to him, but that he has never handled, for a less compensation than he can be persuaded to invest it for, after it has once passed into his effective possession. That this is so is suggested by the growing tendency of joint-stock companies to accumulate reserves out of profits, showing that it is cheaper to provide fresh capital out of undistributed profits than by appealing to the investing public for subscriptions out of profits already distributed.[1]

The tendency of the State to be extravagant as compared with individuals and private corporations and to pile up unproductive debts is not a disproof of what is alleged above, but is due to a different set of causes. In existing society, the State is used by the dominant economic groups to carry out undertakings for their benefit at the expense of other groups. For instance, there are some services which are profitable for capitalist undertaking as a whole, but cannot be made to yield profits to any particular group of entrepreneurs; either the State undertakes to provide them at a loss or it pays to private corporations a subsidy out of public money. Again all States spend a large part of their citizens' income in wars and preparation for wars, among whose real but unavowed objects is often the obtaining of a monopolistic position in certain markets for particular groups of capitalist entrepreneurs that live under the shelter of the State and control its policy.[2]

---

[1] Reserves may either be 'ploughed back' into the business that amassed them or else be invested, directly or through banks and investment trusts, in other businesses. The amount of new capital that is annually provided out of the 'automatic' savings of corporate undertakings is very considerable, and would probably be maintained even at a very low rate of interest.

[2] See R. G. Hawtrey, *Economic Aspects of Sovereignty*.

18. Out of the subjective estimates formed by different persons of goods to be enjoyed at various future dates there emerges, under conditions of free exchange and rights of contract, an objective valuation of future goods. Of course people's time-preferences are very different for different lengths of time and different degrees of remoteness. It does not follow that, if present goods have for me an agio of 5 per cent. over goods available a year hence, they will have an agio of 50 per cent. over goods available ten years hence, or that goods available six years hence will have an agio of 5 per cent. over those available seven years hence. However, as soon as an organised market for Waiting develops, there springs up a class of middlemen in Waiting (banks and investment trusts are typical) who deal indifferently in long- or short-period loans at near or distant dates. Through their mediation there is fixed a definite market rate per cent. per annum independent of individual variations in time-preferences. The process is exactly parallel to the development of Objective Exchange-Value out of Subjective Use-Value. The ratio between the value of present goods, and of goods available after the lapse of unit time (a year) gives the Rate of Interest, the function that commonly expresses objective time-preference. Whereas discount is commonly regarded as derived from interest, the converse is the true nature of the case: interest is derived from the tendency to discount future goods.

19. From the fact that different individuals' subjective time-preferences are various and differ from the objective time-preference expressed in the Rate of Interest it follows that some are willing to lend and some to borrow. Those whose subjective time-preference is less than the market-rate will be willing to lend; those whose subjective time-preference is greater than the market-rate will be willing to borrow. Since the urgency of present needs compared with future ones grows less as income rises, it is, in general, those persons richer than the average that are ready to lend, and those persons poorer than the average that are desirous of borrowing. This identification of lenders and borrowers with rich and poor appears to be contradicted by the fact that entrepreneurs, who are usually wealthy men, operate largely on borrowed money, but this is only an apparent contradiction since entrepreneurs act as the agents of society and borrow not on their own account but on that of the consumers of their wares or on that of the labourers whom they hire; through them the lender makes an advance to consumers or to labourers, who are the ultimate borrowers. Advances to consumers are exemplified in the hiring out of durable consumption-goods; dwelling houses and carriages are traditional cases, but the modern development of hire-purchase has greatly extended this category. Advances to labourers (including salaried workers) are embodied in nearly all wage-payments. The labourer, owing to the greater immediate urgency of his wants, exchanges the goods that his efforts ultimately produce for present goods of equal value but of less physical quantity.[1] In other words, wages are the discounted marginal net product of labour.[2] Another way of putting it is that there are some people willing to convert property into income and others willing to convert income into property (our lenders and borrowers respectively); out of the respective rates at which they are willing to do this (subjective valuations based on time-preference) is formed a rate of interest.[3] But since the wealth of society comes in the form of

[1] This is Böhm-Bawerk's explanation of surplus-value.
[2] This is Taussig's expression (*Principles of Economics*, ch. 52, § 5).
[3] This bears some resemblance to Cassel's view. See his *Nature and Necessity of Interest* and his *Theory of Social Economy*, ch. vi, § 24.

income, only those having a relatively large share of it are in a position to accumulate property; hence again lenders and borrowers tend to be identified with rich and poor.

20. In this form of the theory, interest is explained as a phenomenon of valuation and not of distribution. Once this phenomenon arises, an accumulation of resources becomes of peculiar importance. It renders possible more productive but more roundabout methods of production. (It should be noted that there is no virtue in indirectness alone: it is not that capitalist production is more productive because it makes use of roundabout methods: it is that some roundabout methods are more productive and capitalist production, owing to its command over an accumulation of resources, can make use of these methods.) Work that is not immediately remunerative but that in the long run enhances the productive power of society can be undertaken, and the persons engaged on it can be paid in present goods out of the accumulation. The accumulated resources can thus be reproduced at the end of the period and in addition a surplus product is created. Whoever provides the accumulation, whether the community or private individual, is performing a function that increases value-production; that is to say, is supplying a factor of production. This factor is called Waiting: from the individual standpoint it consists of allowing claims on future goods to mature into claims on present goods; from the social standpoint it consists of refraining from devoting available resources to immediate consumption in order to employ them in more roundabout but more productive ways.

It is the latter view of the process that solves the apparent contradiction between the two views of the nature of capital that are current. One regards capital as

the function of Waiting, the other regards it as a quantity
of resources disposable in production or, more precisely,
as produced means of production. It is the process of
Waiting or Saving that diverts the economic activities of
society from the production of goods required for immediate consumption to the production of instrumental
goods. Thus the result of Waiting is the existence of a
stock of produced means of production, and the return
to Waiting is embodied in surplus-value, i.e. the difference between the value of the goods produced and the
value of the means of production. This difference is the
so-called productivity of capital. The net return to capital
goods is the total return, i.e. the value of the product,
diminished by the cost, i.e. the imputed value of the
instrumental goods. This is the same as the surplus-value
above mentioned. Hence the return to Waiting is identical
with the net marginal product of Capital goods.

Thus both conceptions of Capital, either as Waiting
or as produced means of production, lead to the same
definition of Interest. Waiting however is the more
fundamental conception, since it brings into prominence
the element of time-preference, and it will be adopted
here as the name of this factor of production. This will
not, however, preclude the treatment of the factor at the
same time as a collection of instrumental goods. In effect
the demand for and the supply of Waiting are the same as
the demand for and the supply of produced means of
production.

21. Waiting must thus be considered as a factor of production
and the rate of Interest can be considered from the two
aspects of the demand for and the supply of a function.
The demand for the function is, as in the case of other
factors of production, derived from its marginal net product, which is the same as the marginal net product of

the material objects in which it becomes incorporated. Owing to the law of diminishing returns and to the diminishing marginal utility of first-order goods, the demand price of higher-order goods becomes less as the quantity available increases. Thus the rate of Interest depends on the quantity of accumulated resources; as a community grows richer the rate of Interest tends to fall. This occurs whether the resources are collectively or privately owned and irrespective of distributional conditions in the latter case; it is independent of any changes from the side of supply, due to the effect of augmented income on time-preference.

22. The supply of Waiting depends on the time-preference of the marginal saver. This in turn depends on the total wealth of the community, its existing state of distribution, the prevalent forms of property ownership, and the habits and customs of the people. This last category is a mental lumber-room for unexplained causes, but the first three can be explained in brief. The greater the wealth of the community the greater, *ceteris paribus*, is the provision for present needs and so the lower the marginal saver's time-preference. Thus the richer the community the greater will be the supply of saving at a given rate of interest.

Inequality in private fortunes has two contradictory effects, one tending to diminish, the other to increase the amount of saving forthcoming at a given price. The first of these is that the existence of a class of very rich people tends to set a higher standard of comfort and luxury than prevails in a community of less inequality, thereby diminishing the surplus available for investment. The second is that, owing to the low time-preference of rich people, a rate of interest that would not tempt any savings out of a community of equally circumstanced persons would skim off some of the excess of the largest incomes, were the same sum less equally divided. In the unequal community the number of supra-marginal savers would be more, and the proportion of savings saved above the margin would be greater. Let us compare two countries with the same population and the same total wealth. In the one wealth is unequally divided, in the other equally. If rich people in the inequalitarian country had the same tastes and habits of expenditure as the citizens of the equalitarian country, more savings would be forthcoming at a given price in the first country than at the same price in the second. Puritanism, by restraining idle and wanton expenditure, made inequality conducive to accumulation. Under modern conditions, the prevalence of competitive standards of ostentation among the rich makes it possible that inequality actually reduces the amount of saving possible at a given rate of interest.

The chief influence of the forms of property ownership lies in the different effects of individual and associative property, and in especial of private and public property. As mentioned elsewhere, associative time-preferences are usually lower than individual ones, so that a prevalence of associative, especially public property, over individual property would tend to increase the supply of saving forthcoming at a given price.

23. (ii) *Uncertainty-bearing.*—Closely allied to Waiting on the one hand and to Business Organisation on the other is the function of Uncertainty-bearing. It resembles Waiting in that one of its pre-requisites is the existence of a stock of resources, but the time-element does not enter into it. In practice almost all investment involves both waiting and uncertainty-bearing. Thus the return to Capital is a composite payment, the return partly to one and partly to the other, but there are some investments (stocks of established governments), that involve only Waiting, and it is possible to conceive of Uncertainty-bearing divorced from Waiting.[1] Like the Organisation of Enterprise it involves an element of choice and direction. In fact the ordinary business man is not only an organiser and initiator of economic activity but also one who ventures his own or borrowed resources, being induced to risk loss by the probability of a greater gain.

Owing to the diminishing marginal utility of resources the certainty of one pound has greater subjective value than the equal probability of two pounds or nothing. Thus the exposure of resources to risk involves a loss of utility not measured by the actuarial value of the risked resources and such exposure is only compensated for by a gain greater than that which makes a mathematical equivalent for the loss. This surplus gain increases with the risk run. In other words, if two investments of unequal uncertainty are to be balanced in respect of their subjective values the less certain must have an actuarial value greater than the more certain. Where an organised market exists, out of these subjective estimations there arises a scale of objective prices for the taking of risks. Hence the different rates of yield obtained from different kinds of investments.

24. There are two different kinds of risk, insurable and non-insurable. The essence of insurance is to take advantage of the law of averages applying to large numbers, and by aggregating risks to make them cancel each other. The risks that can be treated in this way are those that are known to conform to the law of averages. Risks that do not so conform can be transferred from one person to another; they can be aggregated and transferred to some-one whose resources are larger and therefore better able to bear the risk than those of the transferrers, but they

[1] See A. C. Pigou, *Economics of Welfare*, Appendix I.

are not thereby destroyed. Insurable risks usually arise from physical and biological causes whose effects are statistically predictable. Uninsurable risks usually arise from psychological causes and include changes in fashion, in the political situation and in the economic conjuncture. Thus it is possible to insure against death, fire and theft, against a wet bank holiday and the loss of a ship at sea. In the aggregate of events there is no risk: there is certainty. But it is impossible to insure (in the strict sense of the word) against a general election, a shortening of women's skirts, or a fall in prices, since in these cases the aggregate of a large number of risks is simply a magnified risk.[1] Thus, when a manufacturer covers himself against price fluctuations by selling futures or by working only to order, the risk is not destroyed, it is only transferred to the buyer of futures or to the merchant who places the order. Someone has to bear it and that someone is usually paid for it in the form of a higher average level of business profit, as compared with the trader who plays for safety. It is this second kind of risk, the non-insurable risk, that the economist has in mind when he counts risk-bearing as one of the factors of production. All production in anticipation of demand involves the risk that the product by the time it reaches the market will have missed the opportune moment for profitable sale. Capitalist production, that is to say the laying down of fixed plant and the establishment of a specialised organisation, increases the quantity of resources exposed to risk and the time for which they are so exposed. The more numerous are the kinds and qualities of goods available to the consumer the greater is the need for Uncertainty-bearing. Stan-

[1] The fact that insurance companies will insure against risks of this sort does not invalidate the distinction drawn above. In doing so they depart from their proper function of risk-destroying and simply assume, without destroying, risks that their large resources enable them to bear.

dardisation can reduce unnecessary risk of this sort, but cannot eliminate all risk without destroying the consumer's freedom of choice. It is only if business men are willing to expose their resources to some measure of risk that any business can be done at all. On the willingness of some entrepreneurs to assume large risks depends the possibility of making progress in industry and trade. The opening up of new markets, the selling of new products, the utilisation of new processes involve the exposure of great resources to considerable risk, assuming of course, average ability and efficiency of the entrepreneur. If the venture is unsuccessful the resources are wholly or partially lost. If it is a success the resources in question yield more than the normal rate of return.

The social importance of Risk-bearing lies in the fact that progress comes through the selection of advantageous variations. Every variation (experiment, enterprise) in economic conditions involves some risk, but the more variations there are the more chances there are that some improvement will emerge. Advantageous variations can be preserved, disadvantageous ones scrapped. Man is playing with Nature a game of 'heads I win, tails you lose'.

The difference between the long-period average return of resources exposed to a given class of risk, and that of resources used in a perfectly safe investment measures the return on the bearing of that class of risk, or the pure Profit. If entrepreneurs in general underestimate the riskiness of a given investment of resources there will be an over-supply in that direction, which may extinguish the premium on risk-bearing—the Profit—altogether.

25. The demand for the function of Uncertainty-bearing is increased by any circumstance that increases the necessary fluctuations in economic activity and diminished by any circumstance that makes for stability. It consequently

depends on a variety of causes. Chief among these may be mentioned:—

(*a*) The number and variety of commodities that are offered for the choice of consumers.

(*b*) The prevalence of changes of fashion and taste among consumers.

(*c*) The prevalence of inventions, new processes, or new methods of organisation.

(*d*) The extent of specialisation in industry—all specialisation involves increased exposure to risk.

(*e*) The extent of the market for goods and consequently the amount of potential competition.

(*f*) The methods of organisation of enterprise— numerous competing business units increase risk, industrial integration reduces it but cannot eliminate it. The chief cause of the instability found under competitive conditions is the mutual ignorance in which competing firms work: each plans for the market or introduces new methods without regard to the similar activities of all the others.

(*g*) The stability of the monetary and financial system.

(*h*) The stability and security of the political organisation.

26. The supply of Uncertainty-bearing depends on the same causes as the supply of Waiting. The wealth of the community, its distribution, the prevalent forms of Property all have a similar influence in the two cases. But the part played by individual temperament is greater here than in the case of Waiting. Individuals otherwise similarly situated differ greatly in their willingness to expose their resources to risk. The supply of Capital is therefore facilitated by devices that enable any individual to associate as much or as little Uncertainty-bearing with a given amount of Waiting as he likes. Among such devices are

the sleeping-partnership; the loan on security; the separation of shares in joint-stock companies into different categories, carrying different degrees of risk and appropriate variations of returns. Such devices make possible a specialisation of function between risk-taking and non-risk-taking investors, which augments the total quantity of potential investment. Examples of similar specialisation are afforded by manufacturers' producing to order and by the hedging on futures referred to above (p. 128). The manufacturer specialises in making goods and passes on the risks of price fluctuation to the merchant who specialises in watching markets.

27. It is worth while remarking that the function of Uncertainty-bearing is not confined to the entrepreneur. The worker, too, bears uncertainty. He runs the risk of unemployment or of fluctuating employment. Generally, the more highly specialised he is the greater is this risk, but it varies much according to the occupation. In a world of perfect individualism, where men knew the wages paid and the chances of employment in all trades, and had equal opportunities of venturing into any trade, these risks would be compensated by wage-differentials. In the actual world there is in some cases a tendency for industries in which wages or employment is more than normally variable to pay higher average wages, but hindrances to mobility are so great that this tendency has only a very intermittent operation. As a rule the worker is insufficiently compensated for fluctuation in earnings.

Owing to the lowness of his income the worker is not in a position to bear uncertainty well and therefore any social arrangements that diminish uncertainty for him are a good thing. Unemployment insurance is one such arrangement. No scheme of insurance can destroy this risk: it can only shift it upon other shoulders, but it may shift it upon shoulders better able to bear it. A system of national unemployment insurance with contributions and benefits at a flat rate, financed by workers, employers and the State, throws the risk partly upon the community as a whole and partly upon entrepreneurs as a whole. It therefore involves the subsidising of the riskier trades by the less risky ones. A scheme of unemployment insurance in which every industry was insured by itself and bore all its own cost would transfer the risk from workers to employers in the same trade. Unemployment insurance by industry would then appear the sounder economic system, but it suffers from the disadvantages of being more complex and more costly to administer and of hindering mobility between trades. The best system of unemployment insurance would seem to be one on a national basis but with a gradation of employers' contributions according to the variability of employment in their particular industries. While unemployment insurance diminishes the amount of uncertainty-bearing that the worker is obliged to supply, producers' co-operation and schemes of profit-sharing or co-partnership increase it and are on that account to be condemned. The worker's interest is best served by standard rates and conditions, common to as many trades over as wide an area as possible. To make a worker's income depend on the prosperity of the particular concern with which he is connected is to introduce an undesirable element of uncertainty into his livelihood.

28. Business profits form a category of income that is hard to classify. In ordinary speech the word Profit covers many forms of income that can manifestly be allotted to other categories. Thus it may include Interest on Capital (pure Waiting) and Rent of Land owned by the business (including differential advantage of location), also Wages of management or superintendence on the part of the business man. These must be excluded before we can deal with true Profit. A test that can be applied to the labour of management is whether it can be delegated or not. Any function that can be delegated to a salaried official is no essential part of the function whose earnings are Profit. The residual part of business profits then appear to consist of four elements. First, there is the return to Uncertainty-bearing (Profit in the narrow sense used here). Second, there is an element due to chance variations in the conditions of business: in a stationary society these would cancel out when summed over the whole field of business, but in a progressive state they are more likely to be positive than negative and thus form part of the income of the business class. Following the German usage we may call these Conjuncture-gains. Third, there are differential gains, analogous to rent, due to permanent advantages that one business has over another, advantage of efficient internal management, of trade marks and patents, and of established custom. Fourth, there are monopoly-gains, due either to deliberately organised monopoly or to mere accidental absence of competition (economic frictions). Many cases of the third kind are practically indistinguishable from the fourth. The first element in profits is the result of the business man's disposal over produced means of production. The second, third and fourth are due to his position as controller of the organisation of industry. They may thus be classed as income due to business organisation.

29. We can conceive of Capital in two ways: either as an historical category, involved in a certain social system and involving certain conditions of organisation and of distribution; or as a technical factor in the process of production, appearing in all stages of development. As an historical category Capital requires for its development a

certain previous degree of accumulation and the institutions of property and contract. In practically all cases
where it has appeared in recent times it has been private
capital, that is to say, the accumulation has been private
property and the function of Waiting has been supplied
by wealthy private persons, who function on behalf of
the community, and appropriate the return to the function,
that is, receive interest on their capital. Owing to the
way in which this institution developed the persons who
provided the capital were also in general those who
directed its use, i.e. who provided the function of enterprise, hence the description of the modern entrepreneur
system as capitalism. It is theoretically possible that the
community as a whole should provide the necessary
Waiting and that the instrumental goods so produced
should be public property. Capital as an historical category
would then be quite different from what it is to-day, but
such a community would still possess Capital in the
technical sense, and in the allotment of its resources to
alternative uses would have to make use of the conception
of a rate of interest, although interest would not be paid
to any individual. (See the Appendix to this Chapter.)

30. III. LAND.

At first sight the propriety of admitting Land as a factor
of production may be called into question. Is it not a
passive thing? Is it right to speak of a return to it, and
is not Rent merely an artificial and unnecessary deduction
from the earnings of human activity? The inclusion of
Land, or, more accurately, of the Uses of Land among
the other factors is, however, necessary if the marginal
system is to be carried out logically. This appears most
clearly from the so-called Differential Theory of Rent,
which shows that there is a difference in the total return
on equal amounts of human activity applied to different

pieces of land. If we are to maintain that the earnings of equal amounts of human activity are equal we must admit the existence of a surplus arising from the qualities of land in question. This surplus is the Rent payable for the use of these qualities of the land. Or, from the point of view of a community endeavouring to get the greatest output of utilities from the resources at its disposal, natural objects and instrumental goods can be substituted for one another at the margin; also the supply of the former is not unlimited so there must be some criterion as to how far it is worth while to apply them. This means that Land has a definite return[1] which must be imputed to it in any accurate costing process. This is the Scarcity Theory of Rent; it emphasises the fact that Land is naturally restricted, so that its return contains an element of surplus. Indeed, since it has no supply price, the whole of its return is surplus. This surplus is identical with the surplus of the Differential Theory. Thus the two theories are strictly compatible with each other; are, in fact, aspects of one theory. In whatever way calculated, the return to Land is a real entity and must appear in the economy of any community. All returns of course are ultimately part of some individual's or corporation's income; the fact that the return to land is not produced by any individual and yet is appropriated by some person or persons is the source of the arbitrariness of Rent alluded to above. The ultimate incidence of Rent among persons is determined by social institutions and so belongs to the subject of Personal Distribution.[2]

---

[1] It is a case of residual value. (See Chapter III, sections 29 and 31.)
[2] E. Cannan (*History of Local Rates in England*, second edition, 1912, pp. 181–182) points out that it is not necessary that Rent should be appropriated by individuals: it might be wiped out by over-cultivation of the superior lands. If this occurred, then Earnings might be higher than before, since transference of labour and capital to the better land would raise the margin of cultivation, but the income

31. The doctrine that the value of each factor of production is equal to its marginal net product is true, but its usefulness is limited. The position of the margin only indicates and does not determine the value of the factor.[1] Marginal net product has become a magic word in the mouths of some theorists, who talk of it as if it were an easily and definitely ascertainable quantity, as constant and as determinable as, say, the efficiency of a transformer. In reality Value and the margin of application are determined concurrently by the same underlying set of causes. These can be divided again into two divisions and entitled demand and supply; but this division is only arbitrary, since a change in the conditions of supply of one factor affects the demand for all other factors. A change in the demand for a factor of production will affect the distribution of income and hence the demand for goods and the supply of other factors of production. A realistic classification of causes tending to affect the margin would group together causes that operate on both the supply and on the demand side. Thus the technical conditions of production affect both the demand and the supply of factors of production. Psychological factors include consumers' tastes on the demand side and workers' preferences on the supply side. The whole conception, instead of solving all problems in distribution, is only a restatement of them. Such restatement is made perhaps in exacter terms and brings us nearer a solution in that way, but that is all.

of the community as a whole would be lowered. To obtain the maximum gross return, some system of ownership and control, public or private, is necessary in order to distribute human effort so as to force cultivation down to the margin. When Oppenheimer (*Grundriss*, § 44) says that in the *freie Genossenschaft* incomes will tend to equality in spite of unequal fertility of soils, the size of the holding adjusting itself naturally in the inverse ratio of its productivity, it is probable that this wiping out of economic rent by over-cultivation is what really would take place.

[1] A. Marshall, *Principles of Economics*, V, viii, 5.

32. The theory of the demand for factors of production has been very fully worked out: it is that part of the doctrine of the Austrian School that has gained most complete acceptance among economists and that has had most influence on social and political thought. The demand-price of a factor is its marginal net product; in other words it pays to continue employing additional units of the factor until the net addition made to the value of the product by the last unit employed is equal to the price paid for the use of the unit. Like all prices, this is a two-dimensional quantity. If the price of a factor be considered as given, the quantity that it is worth while to employ is determined: this is the aspect seen by the individual entrepreneur, combining and substituting factors whose prices are fixed by market conditions beyond his control. On the other hand, given the quantity of the factor available, the price at which it can all be made use of is determined; this is the aspect seen by the social economist.

33. This theory requires to be qualified in two directions.

Firstly, under the social institutions that exist to-day, the entrepreneur function is organised almost entirely on the basis of private enterprise, either of single individuals or of corporations of such. Thus it may happen, and frequently does happen, that the limit to which it is profitable for the entrepreneur to push the utilisation of a factor of production or of factors in general does not coincide with the margin fixed by social demand, as indicated by price. This is due chiefly to three causes: deficient bargaining power of the suppliers of certain factors; monopoly, which restricts production and consequently the employment of all factors; and other causes, usually open or concealed taxes and subsidies, that enable the entrepreneur to employ fewer or more factors than under perfect equilibrium and to pay less or more than their true value for them. These causes may affect single businesses or whole industries. Hence side by side with the true marginal net product or marginal social net product, Professor Pigou distinguishes marginal trade net product and marginal individual net product, to denote respectively the net product of the marginal factor employed profitably by the representative entrepreneur in a given industry or by a given individual entrepreneur.[1]

Secondly, to the degree in which inequality in individual income exists, the social demand schedule, which is developed in the market and which determines prices and margins throughout the social economy, is a distorted measure of real need and real economic welfare.[2]

34. The theory of the supply of factors of production has been comparatively neglected by economists, although it has more immediate bearing than that of the demand for factors on our ultimate problem of personal distribution.

There is the important difference between factors that have and those that have not a definite supply-price. In the first place, a part of the produced instruments of production and the functions of Waiting and Uncertainty-bearing on which their existence depends have a definite supply-price; unless this is paid they are not forthcoming and there is a relation between the price offered and the amount available. But it is probable that some Waiting at least, and possibly a large part, would be forthcoming irrespective of the reward offered. The same applies to much Uncertainty-bearing. Thus this part of the total supply of Capital is governed by the rent-principle. Many kinds of Labour, especially skilled, technical, professional, and administrative work, have a supply-price: if the

---

[1] *Economics of Welfare*, first edition, Part II, ch. vi–viii. In the second edition the terminology is modified, but the same matter is found in Part II, ch. ix–xi.   [2] See p. 79 and p. 86n.

worker does not get the wage which he considers appropriate to the job he will not work. But, except in the case
of workers who have an income from property sufficient
to live on, the worker must work at something. Thus
Labour as a whole has no supply-price. Subject, therefore, to many qualifications, some Capital and some kinds
of Labour have a definite supply-price. On the other
hand, the supply of Land, as defined by the economist,
and that of natural raw materials is a fixed quantity;
the supply of some kinds of labour, including the most
simple and unskilled as well as the work of genius and
inspiration, is not, indeed, a fixed quantity, but one whose
variation appears to be independent of the price offered
for their use. Such factors have no supply-price. (See
Chapter III, section 34, pp. 94–95.)

35. It has been mentioned that causes operating from the
supply-side may shift the margin of profitable application
of a factor, so that although, owing to the formal equality
of demand price and supply price at the exchange point,
the factor is still receiving its marginal net product, this
marginal net product will be a new one, and the operating
cause of this change in value will be a change in the conditions of supply.

Any cause tending to restrict the supply of a factor
whether it be natural restriction (scarcity in conjunction
with irreproducibility) or the action of social institutions
—traditional immobility, caste, class divisions, inheritance,
political privilege, monopoly, etc.—tends in two ways to
increase its return relatively to that of unrestricted or less
restricted factors. In the first place, by creating a scarcity,
it raises the margin of profitable application of the restricted
factor and thus raises its return; in the second place, by
forcing the unrestricted factors into other uses, it lowers
their margin of use and with it their return. The raising

of the return per unit of the restricted factor takes two forms: first, diminishing the number of people from whom the supplies of the factor may be selected and hence lowering both the average efficiency and the marginal efficiency of the factor; second, increasing the competition of consumers for the services of people supplying this factor and hence making these services dear. For instance, supposing entry into the legal profession were restricted to red-headed men, we should have to pay our lawyers higher fees than we do now, because their services would be scarcer. Their services moreover would be on the average less efficient, because among the red-headed lawyers that could remain in practice would be some that would be less efficient than some of the non-red-headed men excluded from the profession. Similar arguments apply conversely to the unrestricted factors. The over-supply of these causes the community to pay less money for the services of persons some of whom, if they had the opportunity, would be capable of work of a higher quality.

36. The fundamental principle in factor distribution is that of rent. Society in the co-operative satisfaction of its needs demands certain factors, and the persons who happen to be in a position to supply them get the return thereon. This is merely another form of the truism that value is derived from demand and not from either labour or sacrifice.

Where economic activities are conducted along traditional lines or where, even given a certain amount of economic rationality, the supply of factors whereby each member of the community gets his livelihood is prescribed and fixed, the rent principle holds immediately of such factors.

Where, however, there exists a sufficient degree of economic rationality, including mobility of persons between

different occupations (the implicit assumptions of orthodox economists), an economic subject adjusts the supply
of the factors that he controls until he is obtaining maximum
economic well-being. This means, among other things,
that he could not get any more by changing the kind or
amount of his output of factors of production. There thus
enters in a still more fundamental form of opportunity-
cost and a still more fundamental unit factor of production,
the unit of opportunity, underlying the other specific
factors. The rent principle still operates, but it applies,
not to any particular factor, but to the units of opportunity. We may consider that so many units of opportunity
are the lot of any particular individual. In the extreme
case of perfect mobility and complete freedom of choice
of occupations, the actual number of units depends on
the individual's natural qualifications, including ability,
interest in work, energy and adaptableness. Thus persons
of equal endowments will tend to secure equal remuneration for equal objective disutilities (or sacrifice of possible
utilities). Social institutions that restrict the income-
getting activities of different individuals to an unequal
degree introduce arbitrary variations in the number of
opportunity-units that fall to the lot of any particular
individual: arbitrary in the sense that they do not depend
on the individual's natural qualifications. In other words,
a particular individual's opportunities are partly a function
of his abilities and partly a function of the social institutions that environ him.

INTEREST IN A SOCIALIST COMMUNITY

Böhm-Bawerk,[1] Wieser,[2] Gustav Cassell[3] and Henderson[4] have maintained the view here expressed as to the necessity of interest, as a book-keeping conception, in a socialist community. Many socialists, who otherwise admit the validity of orthodox economics, dissent from it. It rests on the following grounds.

A community, as well as an individual, has a time-preference. There is a limit beyond which it is not worth while, from the social point of view, to incur further productive expenditure. This limit is a function of the wealth of the community and of the length of time that must elapse before the expenditure in question yields its fruits. Even the richest community cannot afford all the conceivable public works.

Assuming that a certain amount of the community's present resources are ear-marked for capital expenditure, how are they to be apportioned among the possible uses in different industries and different localities? What common measure can be found for, say, the Channel tunnel, the Severn barrage scheme, a London County Council tramway extension, the sinking of new coalpits in Kent, and a drainage-scheme in the Fens? This is a double problem: first, what uses are worth while; second, how much shall be expended on each use. We require a method of accounting that makes comparison possible between different kinds of needs, and between different ways of supplying one need. Such a method must use the concept of value. But when we are comparing the cost of goods required year

---

[1] *Macht oder ökonomisches Gesetz?* (*Gesammelte Schriften*, p. 300.)
[2] *Natural Value*, Book IV, ch. ii and ch. viii.
[3] *Theory of Social Economy*, ch. vi, § 26.
[4] *Supply and Demand*, ch. i, § 5.

by year with that of a quantity laid down once and for all and
yielding their utilities over a period of years, the kind of value
that occurs is not the straightforward value of present goods,
but involves the element of waiting. A method of accounting
that makes use of the concept of interest is the only one that
will comply with these conditions. Similarly, interest must
be reckoned in the depreciation, renewal, and insurance
accounts of all socialistic undertakings.

A socialist society would have to devote a certain proportion
of each year's income to capital uses. It would then have to
fix a rate of interest high enough to reduce the demand for
capital resources to this figure. All collective enterprises, however organised, would have to pay interest to the State for the
use of such resources. This would form part of the income
of the community, to be used either as part of the resources
devoted to further capital uses, or, if it exceeded the necessary amount, distributed in the form of personal income.
This is not to say that some expenditure would not have to
be determined by the method of rationing (as at present):
for example, that on defence, education, fine art, etc., but
expenditure on this method ought to be reduced to a
minimum and taken out of the general fund before calcu-
lating the rate of interest to be charged for productive
investments.

The objection that it is merely paying out of one pocket
and into another is without weight. All large corporations
take account of interdepartmental transactions, otherwise waste
would accrue. A co-operative bank or credit institute charges
interest to its members, whether societies or individuals, for
advances made to them, although such interest returns, in the
form of dividends, to the members. This is necessary in order
to deal fairly as between one member and another. Advances
are made to them individually; dividends are paid to them
collectively. All book-keeping and costing is the division of
one big money-bag into many little pockets, and the detailing

of every transfer between them.[1] Efficient socialist economy is only possible if every undertaking and portion of an undertaking is made to stand on its own accounting feet, and if book-keeping, costing and statistical returns proceed along the same lines as those of capitalist corporations.

The final argument in favour of the use of interest is provided by the character of the alternative methods suggested of providing capital for public enterprises and apportioning it between them. One favourite scheme is that of 'considering each scheme on its merits' by means of boards and committees, on the lines of the compulsory economy (Zwangswirtschaft) of war-time, the 'Zentrale' of post-war Germany and the 'Glavki' of revolutionary Russia during the period of military communism. Although such bodies may have their uses, they are rather as organs of information and investigation than as balancers of competing claims. The problems are too complicated to be dealt with in this way (consider the examples quoted on page 142). The records of the bodies just named are a sufficient objection to their general use in this way.

Another scheme suggested is that every industry should provide its own capital out of surplus. But then the amount of capital that an industry could command would be measured, not by the social need thereof, but by the elasticity of the demand for its products. Hence vineyards would displace corn-fields in all regions where both grape and wheat will grow. No socialised industry should show a surplus. The principle of maximising economic welfare by pushing production everywhere to the margin, demands that goods be sold at cost (including salaries, interest, insurance and cost of marketing). A surplus can only arise, (a) through the exercise of monopoly power, (b) through windfalls. But in the first case it is a concealed tax on a particular commodity. If it is desired to raise revenue in this way it should be done openly and by a definite, fixed tax, and the proceeds should go to the

[1] Henderson, *Supply and Demand*, ch. iv, § 2, 3.

general treasury. In the second case, too, unforeseen and non-recurring sources of income not due to any action of the industry should belong to the commonwealth (which should, and in the last resort must, provide for losses incurred in the same way).

CHAPTER V

THEORY OF PERSONAL DISTRIBUTION

1. The income of an individual is the sum of a number of terms each equal to the product of two quantities, first the number of units of a factor of production that he has the disposal of, and second the yield per unit of such factor.[1] According to the method that has become traditional in Great Britain attention is chiefly concentrated on the second of these quantities: in fact the discussion of distribution in some works on economics is entirely confined to this subject. Such a theory of distribution says nothing directly about any individual's total income. It indicates only the return on a unit of a given factor and is silent as to the number of units of any factor or as to the different

---

[1] This way of formulating income tacitly assumes some common measure in terms of which different factors can be expressed. Since money is the only possible measure, it implies the commodity nature of factors of production and the existence of some method of valuing them, such as that of net marginal products. It also accords with the suggestion, made at the end of the preceding chapter, of the existence of one fundamental factor of production: opportunity. The statement would then read 'the income of an individual is equal to the product of the number of units of opportunity at his disposal into the average yield of one such unit'. The concept of 'opportunity' is a vague one, but no more so than Pigou's generalised commodity 'wheat' (*Essays in Applied Economics*, Essay XVI, 'The Exchange Value of Legal-Tender Money'). There is an analogy between the method there adopted of subsuming all commodities under one and the method used here of subsuming all factors under one. In both cases the formation of price is assumed. We can express these statements symbolically as follows:

$$I = \Sigma np = N\bar{p}$$

where I = total income, n = the number of units of a particular factor of production and p = its yield, N = the number of units of opportunity and $\bar{p}$ = the average yield of an opportunity-unit.

kinds of factors that may be at the disposal of any particular person. Our analysis of this quantity has shown
that it is equal to the marginal net product of the factor in
question, but far from exhausting the subject it has directed
our attention away from the demand for the factor, on
which the writers of the productivity school chiefly con-
centrate, to the supply of the factor.

2. Our discussion of the supply of factors of production has
drawn attention to the element of opportunity, and the
influence of social institutions in modifying the supply of
factors and hence the incomes of persons supplying them.
We have seen that under conditions of equality of opportunity the returns on equal natural abilities would tend
to be equal. Under actual social systems these conditions
only partly hold good. All persons do not enjoy equal
opportunities. Their start in life depends on nutrition,
education, and initial capital; these in turn depend on
the pecuniary position of their parents. Their subsequent
progress is conditioned by their legal and social status, by
the amount of their property, by their opportunity of
entering different occupations, and by the organisation of
enterprise and the system of rules regarding property and
contract in vogue in the society they live in. Society is
usually divided into groups, so that within each group
considerable equality of opportunity is enjoyed by its
constituent members, whereas no such equality exists
between members of different groups. These groups may
be called, using a phrase coined by Cairnes[1] and revived
by Taussig,[2] 'non-competing groups'.

The bases for separation into non-competing groups are

---

[1] J. S. Cairnes, *Leading Principles of Political Economy*, Part I,
ch. iii, § 5.
[2] F. W. Taussig, *Principles of Economics*, ch. 46, § 6, Vol. II, pp. 141–
144.

very various. As we have already seen (Chapter II, sections 34 and 37) difference of race or sex forms a basis for very sharp discrimination. Castes and orders, as defined in Chapter II (sections 30–33) form non-competing groups with varying degrees of clear definition. In a society based on the institutions of economic freedom and of private property in the means of production, there often develops (as we shall show later, there tends inevitably to develop) a division into classes which form non-competing groups that are none the less real for having their lines of demarcation somewhat indistinct. Such a society is divided into groups, defined roughly by income-limits and more precisely by opportunities of obtaining education and control over capital; members of the same group have considerable mobility and free choice of occupation within certain limits that are characteristic of the groups, whereas movement from one group to another is much more restricted.

The term 'non-competing groups' is not, perhaps, a happy one, since the groups, as groups, may compete with one another. For example, unskilled workers in conjunction with automatic machines may compete with skilled workers in conjunction with simpler machines, or in a caste-society smiths as a group are in competition with potters as a group, since some utensils may be made either of metal or of clay. What is implied by the term in question is that each group is formed of persons who compete with each other for a livelihood within the group but that persons of different groups do not compete with one another as individuals. In the same examples, unskilled workers do not compete for the same jobs as skilled ones; if the public take to using earthen vessels unemployed smiths cannot compete with potters in the pottery trade.

3. Under existing conditions in Great Britain we may distinguish five main groups, defined partly by size of

income and partly by source of income. The enumeration
differs from Taussig's principally in dividing the very rich
from the middle-class, and in dividing the working-class
into two instead of into three sections. Other divisions could
be made; the actual number and composition of the groups
is of less importance than the admission of their existence, and the recognition of important exceptions to the
occupational mobility assumed by orthodox economists.
Since these groups correspond to what are usually recognised as 'social' classes, we will designate them by their
currently used names. These names must not be taken as
more than mere labels: no significance must be attributed
to the words 'upper' or 'lower' other than that of 'richer'
or 'poorer'; nor must the name 'working class' be held
to imply that no members of the other groups ever do any
work. The five chief groups are:—

(1) Upper Class: deriving income almost exclusively
    from property and large-scale enterprise; large
    property owners (land or securities) and industrial
    magnates, exceptionally gifted artists, writers and
    professional men.

(2) Upper Middle Class: drawing income from property,
    enterprise and intellectual labour; small property-
    owners, proprietors of moderate-sized (usually com-
    petitive) businesses, averagely competent members
    of the learned professions and public services. On
    the whole, this group is composed of those who can
    reasonably hope to reach the £1,000 a year mark but
    not to pass much farther.

(3) Lower Middle Class: composed of petty property-
    owners (who must usually work as well as own),
    owners of small businesses and persons performing
    intellectual work not requiring much training or
    responsibility, typical members being clerks and
    small shopkeepers.

(4) Skilled Working Class: drawing income from work and not at all, or only to a small extent from property, composed of persons performing work that, though not usually reckoned intellectual, requires skill (acquired by vocational training), mental alertness and responsibility.

(5) Unskilled Working Class: drawing income entirely from work and unspecialised, unskilled labour at that, a residual group including not only unskilled workers, but the failures and economic misfits of society, a category into which a skilled worker is very easily thrown by even a short spell of unemployment, sickness or bad luck.

Other distinguishing features are, that groups (1) and (2) usually receive a public school and University education or its equivalent: group (3), a secondary-school, and groups (4) and (5), an elementary-school education. The habit of life insurance appears in the fourth and becomes usual in the higher groups. The habit of saving and investing appears spasmodically in group (4) and is characteristic of all the higher groups. It is very common in the fifth group for both unmarried and married women of the family to work for wages outside the home, and in the fourth group for unmarried women so to work; but in the other groups they do not as a rule do so as a matter of economic necessity, though they may do so for pocket-money, for love of some particular work, or to obtain independence. Leisure is, naturally, co-ordinated with size of income. Thus, in the four groups that habitually work for gain, hours of labour increase progressively from the second to the fifth. Members of group (1) may be said to enjoy one long holiday, those of groups (2) and (3) usually get definite holidays, with pay if they are employed, while those of groups (4) and (5) get what they can or are obliged to take, and are only paid for time actually worked.

4. Ultimately, the composition of a group and the opportunities enjoyed by a typical member of it depend on the institutions of Property (including Contract and Inheritance), Education, and Economic Freedom. The distribution of wealth between members of each non-competing group follows the orthodox theory of marginal productivity. Distribution as between the groups is comparable to that taking place under the laws of international exchange: in other words, the rent-principle holds good, as described at the end of the preceding chapter.

Under these conditions the number of opportunity-units that can be ascribed to any particular person depends partly on natural endowments and partly on opportunities created or restricted by institutions. This can be most clearly seen by abstracting the institutional factor, as can be done by considering individuals belonging to a section of the community that enjoys very high mobility between its various occupations. People of the middle class obtain composite incomes from various sources: work, enterprise, property; but equal abilities and equal efforts tend to produce equal incomes irrespective of their actual sources. Similarly in any particular section of the working class, say among labourers or among artisans, real wage-rates tend to a uniform level whatever the trade or whatever the method of payment (day or week, time or piece). On the other hand, the difference between the average incomes of a doctor and of a docker cannot be referred to the same causes as explain the difference between two doctors of different degrees of skill or industry. To some extent the former difference is due to the institutional factors that make a medical education accessible only to a few even of those who possess the mental and moral qualifications for it.

5. These non-competing groups are the crux of the theory

here set forth. The theory can be attacked in two ways, first by denying the existence of the groups, second by admitting their existence but denying their institutional basis.

6. The first set of objections is directed against the very idea of such stratification in our existing society and asserts that there is complete mobility between all ranks and free choice of occupation for all potentially qualified persons within it.

The existence of some mobility, even of considerable mobility, no one will deny: our society is not rigidly divided into orders or castes like that of old Japan and that of modern India. Nevertheless common experience suggests that there is a difference between the mobility with which a business or professional man settles down into that place in the scale to which his capabilities entitle him and that which permits an exceptionally gifted child of the slums to penetrate into those exalted circles. No one denies that a poor boy (less easily a poor girl) can climb up the business ladder to the independent control of an enterprise, or can win his way to a university education and subsequently to a professional post of honour and emolument. What is asserted here is that to do so he must be a great deal better equipped than the boy from the better-to-do classes who achieves the same goal.

Mobility may be of all degrees: there is the kind that may be pictured by two narrow-necked vases with a thin communicating pipe, and there is the kind that may be pictured by two swamps at different levels. In one case the equalisation of marginal equivalents may be effected by a transference of resources small in comparison with the total magnitudes concerned and may take place very quickly; in the other case the transference required may be large and may proceed very slowly. The existence of non-competing groups is not invalidated by any degree of mobility, however small, but only by a degree of mobility large enough to ensure full equality of opportunity. To take an analogy, a seller may enjoy some monopoly revenue, though not the maximum amount, without having a perfectly closed market: if the barriers exclude only some potential competitors he will be able to draw some benefit from his protected position. In the same way, members of a non-competing group, although subject to the competition of exceptional persons from less-advantaged groups, enjoy an economic benefit due to their freedom from the competition of persons from lower groups who are at least as competent as those members of their own groups who compete effectively with them.

Attempts have been made to investigate this matter statistically; some of these will be discussed in the Appendix to this Chapter (pp. 181–185). Their general conclusion confirms the existence of such groups.

7. The second set of objections to the theory admits the existence of non-competing groups but denies that the barriers between them are due to institutions. Usually it asserts that they are due to innate differences in quality between human beings. The fact that membership of these groups tends to be hereditary, that a man tends to remain in the group he is born into, is attributed to the existence of stocks of congenitally varying efficiency: in short, people are stratified economically according to their innate ability. This view is invalidated not only by general considerations but by many facts of experience. In general, little is known about the unit-characters in the inheritance of mental qualities. There is insufficient evidence to justify the assumption that specific abilities of a socially adapted or economically valuable kind are transmitted from parent to offspring. In different societies the basis of

division into non-competing groups has been so various
that it would be a hardy disputant who would assert that,
whereas in all other societies social divisions were arbitrary, in ours alone social stratification followed along lines
of innate ability. This would be easier to maintain if our
competitive individualism had arisen in a society previously
class-less; but the fact that it has grown up out of the
ruins of a system of Orders and considerable civil inequality, makes it inherently all the less likely. Individuals
of lower classes, given opportunities of development, can
and do rise into higher classes. A sudden windfall, such
as a legacy from a collateral, a big prize in a newspaper
competition, or a favourable and unexpected business
conjuncture, will enrich a family belonging to the lower
middle or labouring class and in two generations its
scions are indistinguishable from those of families who
'arrived' generations earlier. Similarly, an anti-windfall,
such as the death of a breadwinner, the failure of an unlimited liability company or a prolonged and expensive
lawsuit, will thrust a family over the frontier of its group
into a lower one. Among the dregs of society can be found
people who were born to power and wealth. Moreover,
families ramify so extensively that we would find both
lords and labourers, criminals and divines among the
sixty-four great-great-great-great-grandparents of most
persons of whatever class. (This mixture is especially
facilitated by the great prevalence, at some periods, of
bastardy.) A degree of mobility insufficient by far to break
down the barriers between groups is enough to overthrow
the contention of hereditary fitness and unfitness. The only
positive evidence adduced in favour of this view is that of
intelligence tests among elementary school-children and
secondary school-children, which tests are alleged to have
proved the average superiority in raw intelligence of the
latter. However, these tests have been seriously criticised

and it does not appear that any tests have yet been devised that eliminate differences due to nutrition, home environment, and pre-scholastic education.

8. Non-competing groups, both those referred to here and those dealt with by the familiar theory of International Exchange, are maintained as such by barriers that obstruct mobility between them. These may be listed under three heads: (1) ignorance of opportunities, (2) cost of movement, (3) social institutions. International Exchange is chiefly affected by the first two. As between groups in the same community the first two, although they may cause deviations from the normal in the case of a few individuals' incomes (they are dealt with by Pigou as one of the forms of 'friction' impeding the full functioning of the marginal principle), are not important as generators of non-competing groups. When they are, it is, as a rule, in cases that might equally well be classed under the third head. For example, ignorance of opportunities affecting large numbers of people is usually the result of a system of Education. The costs of training for a profession are really one aspect of the institution of Property. A fourth kind of barrier suggests itself: physical force. However, force can rarely be effective unless it has some social sanction behind it, that is, unless its use is part of a social system and it then becomes an incident in the working of some institution, as the police-force is of Property and systematic sabotage of some forms of Labour Organisation. It is thus with the institutional causes of non-competing groups that we shall here deal.

9. The theory here put forward is that certain social institutions or sets of social institutions maintain the existence of non-competing groups, and secure for the more favoured of these groups an Institutional Restriction of certain

factors of production, that the resultant limitation of supply causes their marginal net products to be high relative to those of unrestricted factors, and that there is thus introduced into the earnings of members of the restricted group an element akin to net monopoly revenue. This element in income might be called net Institutional Restriction revenue, but it is proposed to term it shortly Institutional Revenue.

10. Let us consider *seriatim* the chief classes of factors of production and their respective returns.

11. I. LABOUR—WAGES

(Under Wages are included salaries and the earnings of the self-employed worker.) In the remuneration of some kinds of labour, such as that of the highly skilled workman and professional man there is an element of Institutional Revenue. One cause of this is that, where long and costly training is required (as an apprenticeship or a university education), or where the unit of professional activity is an indivisible combination of capital and labour (as a doctor's practice), or where (as in the case of a barrister) the beginner must be prepared to exercise his profession for some years without earning a livelihood, the supply of entrants is limited to persons disposing of accumulated resources.

A second cause is the limitation of supply effected by trade or professional combinations through such devices as demarcation rules, regulation of number of apprentices, or prohibition of labour-saving methods. The enforcement of an abnormally high minimum wage, salary or scale of fees falls into this category, since such enforcement may prevent the inflow from other occupations of persons willing and able to work at a rate which might be higher that what they were already receiving but lower than that enforced by the combination. In all these cases the trade or professional combination must be able to make its rules effective. In some cases this is done by legal enactment (in other words a combination of Political Organisation with Labour Organisation); in other cases by collective bargaining, whereby the fear of having their entire supply of labour withdrawn makes employers acquiesce in rules that limit the number of workmen that they employ and raise the labour cost of production. Where there is already a tendency for entry into an occupation to be restricted by a property qualification, the professional combination need not be formally organised. A tacit agreement among a considerable proportion of employers and persons in whose hands appointment to office lies may produce all the effects of the most powerful trade-union.

Other kinds of institutional restrictions, exemplified in the Oriental and medieval gild-systems and the Indian caste-system, give an Institutional Revenue to members of certain protected occupations. In these cases social institutions have produced an almost complete fixity of supply. The legal or traditional exclusion of women from many occupations is one of the causes of the inferiority of women's wages to men's: in other words, men, as members of a sex, enjoy an Institutional Revenue. Racial discrimination may, in like manner, create Institutional Revenue for the favoured race.

In all these cases, the limitation of the supply of labour to any occupation by a qualification whether of property, of inheritance, of sex, of race, or of anything else save technical competence, acts in two ways. Qualitatively, it narrows the field of selection and thereby diminishes the probability of getting the most efficient service; quantitatively, by restricting the application of the labour force that is available to the more urgent uses only, it raises the marginal net product of that labour. The urgency of the need of the rest of the community for these services is intensified and hence, even without any deliberate formation of a monopoly, any member of an occupation so protected can exchange the product of an hour of his labour against that of more than one hour of other people's labour.

12. We must here discuss a question that was raised but left unsolved in the preceding chapter, namely, whether Labour can be paid at a rate below its marginal net product. Most economists (especially those of the productivity school) assume that on the whole Labour does, in most cases, get its 'natural wage'. Some economists, however, hold that labour can be underpaid or exploited in the sense of getting less than its marginal net product. (This use of the word exploitation is not the same as that of the Marxians, who mean by it any appropriation whatever of rent, interest or profit.) Such exploitation may occur temporarily, for Labour as a whole or for any particular section of labour, in two cases. One is when general prices rise more quickly than money wages; the other is when changes in the economic conjuncture (rise in price of products, fall in the price of co-operant factors) raise the real marginal net product of Labour without a corresponding rise in money wages.

According to the theory of a perfect competitive society any such underpayment would provide employers with an incentive to increase their output until they began to compete for the supply of labour, thereby raising its price to the marginal net product. Thus the labourer could not receive less than his ideal marginal net product. Can permanent underpayment or exploitation exist? If it does some sort of Restriction must occur. Taking first of all the possibility of exploitation in particular trades or in the employment of particular kinds of labour, this Restriction

may be of two forms, ordinary commercial monopoly
or the Restriction of the entrepreneur-function. In the
first case there must not only be monopoly but there must
be no alternative employment for the workman in non-
monopolised trades: otherwise workmen will leave the
trade until employers are obliged to pay the normal rate.
In other words, the employer must have not only a seller's
monopoly but also a buyer's monopoly with respect to
labour. The case is then one of divergence between social
and trade marginal net product: from the point of view
of the particular trade concerned, the workman is getting a
marginal *trade* net product. In the second case the underpayment can only continue if entry into the ranks of the
employing class is limited. Then the comparative scarcity
of entrepreneurs will raise their value and lower that of
workmen. The latter will still be getting the marginal net
product of his labour under prevailing conditions but not
the marginal social net product appropriate to an ideal
competitive system.

Taking now the possibility of exploitation of Labour
in general, our two cases fuse into one, for general monopoly (see Chapter IV, section 13) is the same thing as
Institutional Restriction of the function of business enterprise.

Pigou[1] points out that lack of mobility produces a region
of indeterminateness at any point within which a stable
wage-bargain may be made, the actual point depending on
the relative bargaining powers of the parties. This is the
only precise significance that can be given to the phrase
'inequality in bargaining power' that is so often given in
these discussions as a cause of underpayment (or overpayment of labour). The lack of mobility referred to may
be either as between labourers (due to ignorance, cost of
movement, etc.) or as between labourers and employers.

[1] *Economics of Welfare*, Part III, ch. ix, xiii.

In either case there must be Restriction of the factor of Enterprise, or the unfavourable situation could not be maintained. Such underpayment does not always benefit the employer in the form of surplus profits: sometimes it benefits all employers in a trade or the employing class as a whole by enabling persons who would otherwise be below the margin of efficiency to keep in business and make a living. In all these cases there is a subsidy to employers by workpeople. The workman may be said to be receiving a marginal net product, calculated with reference to the particular circumstances, but this marginal net product is less than the ideal marginal net product. In all these cases there must be Institutional Restriction and therefore the surplus earnings of employers can be regarded as Institutional Revenue.

13. The same analysis may be applied to the far less common case of the payment of Wages above the marginal social net product of labour. This can only occur when the receivers of such wages form a definite group, enjoying a Restriction of their function. The overpayment of particular (usually small) groups of workers, protected by legal privileges or powerful organisation is a possibility. Generally speaking, a trade-union can only raise the wages of a section of workers above their normal level if it can restrict entry into a trade. For the higher earnings make the occupation more desirable and tend to attract new entrants to the trade. If this inflow is not stemmed there are then more men seeking work than can be absorbed at the inflated rate of wages. There will then be either competition of workmen, which will tend to drive wages down, or a permanently high level of unemployment, which means lower real wages. If, however, the inflow can be limited, by apprenticeship restrictions, legislative enactment, trade-union rules, and the like, then an

Institutional Restriction of the supply of that particular kind of labour is effected.

Can workers in general receive more than the marginal social net product of their services? This occurs temporarily in two cases. One is when general prices fall more rapidly than money wages, so that real wages rise without a corresponding increase in productivity. The other is when the economic conjuncture changes unfavourably to the employer (fall in price of products, rise in price of co-operant factors) without a downward revision of wages, so that the marginal net product falls below the wage actually received. But these situations are remedied either by a fall in wage rates or by an increase in unemployment. Can all workers be permanently overpaid? If this occurred it would imply that the working class formed a privileged group enjoying a Restriction of the factor of Labour. It is hard to imagine such a state of affairs, but it might exist temporarily during periods of acute social change, when, for example, employers might keep their establishments going at a loss or employ more men than they could profitably find work for rather than risk revolts of unemployed workmen. Such extra income above the marginal social net product would be Institutional Revenue of the class as a whole. A similar state of affairs exists when wages are kept by any means above their economic level and the resultant permanently unemployed workmen are maintained out of public money. In this case, however, the Institutional Revenue appears not as Wages, but as Income from Civil Rights (see section 19).

14. Before quitting the subject of the earnings of Labour, we must say something about the return to the functions of Business Organisation and of Government. (Cf. Chapter IV, section 9.)

15. (a) *Business Organisation.*—The returns to business enterprise, even after allowance is made for the cancelling of gains by losses, contain an element of Institutional Revenue, and this for two reasons. Firstly, in so far as costly training is required for the making of a business man the supply is limited to such as can afford it. It appears that in proportion as one gate is opened to the moneyless man, through opportunities of joint-stock enterprise, another is being shut, by reason of the growing demand for expensively trained employees to fill positions of responsibility and the tendency to restrict to such men promotion to the highest-paid posts. Even when no costly training is required, personal and family connections usually give to aspirants coming from certain charmed circles advantages that seriously lessen the chances of less-favoured competitors. Secondly, the possession of capital in addition to organising ability is generally necessary in order to start in business. In spite of opportunities for the man without means, due to cheap credit, joint stock enterprise under salaried managers, etc., this is true of the representative firm, and the greater the scope of the enterprise the more the enterpriser requires to be backed by his own capital. When an enterprise is joint-stocked and put under a salaried manager a part of the earnings of management are skimmed off and appropriated by the original owners of the concern or by the promoters. This is the institutional element in those earnings.

We now see why, in popular consideration, the 'entrepreneur' is often called the 'capitalist', in spite of the fact that, economically, he is a specialised kind of labourer. Firstly, he is often a true capitalist as well as an entrepreneur, combining two functions in one person; even where this is not so he belongs, in general, to the same non-competing groups as most capitalists. Secondly, the share of Enterprise, like that of Capital but unlike that of Labour, can be capitalised and become fluid and interchangeable with other kinds of titles to Income from Property. (See section 23.)

16. *Monopoly-Profits.*—Closely connected with the earnings of enterprise is the net monopoly revenue that arises from monopoly in the narrow sense. Although capitalised and merged in the income due to capital and enterprise proper, it is not, like them, due to the supply of any factor of production that has any necessary cost or assignable marginal net product. Even upholders of the productivity theory recognise it as a purely institutional revenue. Yet nowadays it becomes increasingly difficult in practice, if it has not become impossible, to distinguish it from the normal earnings of business enterprise.

17. (*b*) *Government.*—Nowadays public authorities—states and municipalities—maintain a monopoly of this function and supply its services at cost: that is, they exercise it so that no Institutional Revenue accrues from this source to any class of persons. The income of highly placed civil servants may contain an element of Institutional Revenue, but this is by virtue of their belonging to a class which maintains an Institutional Restriction of the supply of all kinds of professional labour. Institutional Revenue derived from the performance of governmental functions as such has been abolished nearly everywhere by the liberal democratic state. Under the feudal system, however, Government was provided, as Enterprise is now, by individuals who made out of it what they could; since these individuals belonged to a privileged order, its supply was the Institutional Restriction of a class.

18. In apparent opposition to this view of the revenue of the state and of the feudal lord is the theory of 'income

of sovereignty' (Herrschaftseinkommen) of some economists of the German sociological school (e.g. Oppenheimer). According to them this category of income, as
also certain forms of monopoly-revenue (capitalist monopolists') and of income from civil rights, is due simply to
appropriation by superior physical force, organised either
by an individual or by a class through the machinery of
the state. This view is too naïve: physical force can explain
neither the political phenomena of tyranny nor the economic phenomena of monopoly-income and sovereignty-
income. The force upon which the tyrant or the capitalist
ultimately relies is that of the very people whom he
oppresses and exploits: hence tyranny or monopoly, to
be more than transitory phases, must be founded in something more organic to the structure of society than the
brute force of the mailed fist or of the policeman's trun-
cheon. Just as in the ultimate analysis all government,
even despotism, is by the consent of the governed,[1] so are
all forms of income due to institutions that are acquiesced
in because none better can be devised and worked at the
time. The so-called incomes of sovereignty are rooted in
institutions that, together with the force that maintains
them, correspond to a particular state of social development. Thus, if the analysis be only carried deep enough,
there is no contradiction between this explanation and
that embodied in the phrase Institutional Revenue.

One form often taken by Income of Sovereignty is that
obtained by the use of coercion to enforce a one-sided
wage-bargain. Such coercion (a particular case of 'inequality of bargaining power') may be either illegal (the
Colorado Coal War of 1914) or legal (Combination Laws).
The one-sidedness is usually unfavourable to labourers,
but may be unfavourable to employers. This could happen
if employers were forced (by law or by terrorism) not only

[1] Cf. J. R. Seeley, *Introduction to Political Science*, Lecture VIII.

to pay a given wage but to employ so many men and to remain in business as employers. In this way a transference could be effected from employers to labourers that could be classified as income of sovereignty and would certainly be Institutional Revenue. Here also, mere coercion is not of itself a sufficient cause of a certain income-distribution. The use of force is a mere consequence of a mere deep-rooted institutional situation. There must first be some Restriction, based on an institution or a complex of institutions, that produces or tends to produce an income for a group; force protects the institution and stabilises the situation it creates. Force may guarantee but it cannot create an income.

19. This also appears to be the place to consider the category of income first distinguished by Dr. Dalton and described by him as 'Income from Civil Rights',[1] namely, income guaranteed by the community to an individual, either unconditionally or under certain conditions, but not as remuneration for services performed. Lord Nelson's perpetual pension is an example of the unconditional kind, an old-age pension one of the conditional kind. This category certainly does not fall within the four corners of the traditional Wages, Interest, Profit and Rent. Does it fit any better into our new classification?

Income from civil rights seems to belong to two cases theoretically distinct but practically confused, according as it involves a redistribution of income solely among members of one non-competing group or according as it involves a transference from one group to another. It may happen that by voluntary co-operation, such as mutual insurance, members of a particular non-competing group may decide to pool part or all of their income and redistribute it (usually according to need). If they do this by

[1] H. Dalton, *The Inequality of Incomes*, Part III, ch. iii, §2.

collective action involving the use of the state, a right to income under certain circumstances is created. This is income from civil rights. A scheme of family endowment or of health insurance contributed to solely by the persons drawing the benefits is an example of this kind. It does not alter its nature if persons of different non-competing groups belong to it, provided the actuarial basis of the scheme does not involve transference. For instance, if contributions and benefits are both on a flat rate or both proportionate to average income, no transference is involved.

The second kind of income from civil rights is that which involves a transference between non-competing groups. This may be either a transference from poor to rich, such as the perpetual pensions and sinecures of the *ancien régime*, paid for out of taxation and enjoyed by an untaxed class, or it may be from rich to poor, such as health insurance or unemployment insurance contributed to by propertied taxpayers[1] and enjoyed by workmen, or such as free education equally available to all and paid for out of rates and taxes roughly proportioned to income. This is really a form of 'income of sovereignty': a politically powerful group is able to dip its fingers into the general revenues of the state and help itself at the expense of less powerful groups.

Obviously civil-rights income is institutional: whether it involves Institutional Revenue or not depends upon its nature. If it is a mere redistribution of income inside a non-competing group that does not create a new such group, then it involves Institutional Revenue or not according as the original income of that group involved Institutional Revenue or not: if it is a transference due to the exercise of sovereignty, then it involves Institutional

[1] The employers' contribution is not relevant here, since its ultimate incidence is on the workman. It adds to labour cost and so tends to lower wages.

Revenue if the particular kind of exercise of sovereignty in question creates an Institutional Restriction.

Of the civil-rights income enjoyed by the working class in the way of education and insurance there are, however, two possible explanations: one is that it is an income of sovereignty, as mentioned above, an increased share in the social swag due to its increased economic and political power or a sop thrown to it by the erstwhile dominant classes; the other is that it is really civil rights of the first kind; the workers, having become entitled by the increased productivity of their labour-power to an increased share in distribution, collectively prefer to take it in the form of civil rights rather than in higher individual wages, thus effecting redistribution within one group rather than any transference.

20. II. CAPITAL.

(a) *Waiting—Interest.*—Although the saving on which the accumulation of capital goods depends is a factor of production that has a supply-price, yet institutional conditions affect not only the amount of saving but also the magnitude of the necessary price, and the number and nature of the recipients of that price. Under existing conditions of private property and free enterprise our chronically spendthrift society turns over into individual hands a large part of the social product that is needed for further productive uses (i.e. the formation of new capital), and then proceeds to tempt it back into these uses by the offer of Interest. This has two effects. Firstly, the provision of this factor is confined in a very large measure to a comparatively small propertied class and the fewer there are to provide a service the higher is the net marginal product of that service and the return per person for providing it. Secondly, every pound saved is remunerated at a rate fixed by the time-preference of the marginal saver, which itself is probably higher than that of the community as a whole would be if it never distributed to individuals the wealth required for future production.[1] Thus is created an Institutional Restriction of the function of Waiting, so that not only does every supra-marginal saver get a saver's surplus, but even the marginal saver is receiving an institutional surplus. Hence a portion of all Interest must be considered as Institutional Revenue.

21. (b) *Uncertainty-bearing—Profit.*—The closely allied function of uncertainty-bearing is subject to a similar criticism. Profit contains an element of Institutional Revenue for three reasons. Firstly, a large part of the uncertainty is created by the competitive-individualistic organisation of economic activity, especially by the mutual ignorance of entrepreneurs. Secondly, the bearing of it is limited under a system of private property and free enterprise to those with resources to expose, that is, to the rich. Thirdly, the same probability of loss, though compensated at the same rate, involves a smaller loss of utility to the richer man than to the poorer. Thus a portion of those earnings of Capital that are due to Uncertainty-bearing must be considered as Institutional Revenue.

22. III. LAND—RENT.

Pure economic theory explains how scarcity and differential rent arise, but since Rent—the return to unproduced means of production—is not a supply-price it stands on a different footing to interest—the return to produced means of production—and there is no purely economic reason for its individual appropriation, even under a system of economic individualism and private property in the produced means of production. The fact is that, with the development of the institution of private

[1] See Chapter IV, p. 120.

property, society validates the claim of the first occupier or last successful stealer of a piece of land to the economic rent thereof. Ownership of natural resources is, because of the comparative fixity of their supply, the purest example of restriction. Thus, on the basis of a natural restriction, an institutional restriction is set up. Individual income drawn from such ownership is an institutional creation, and since it is vested in a limited number of privileged persons, it falls entirely into the category of Institutional Revenue.

23. *Capitalisation of Income.*—One aspect of the rate of Interest which we have considered is that of a ratio between a lump sum and an annual income. As soon as regular channels for the investment of Capital are developed, any sum of money can be changed into an annuity, and conversely any regular annual source of income can be considered as equivalent to a capital sum. Hence income arising from ownership of land and natural materials (rent and royalties) or from business enterprises that enjoy either monopoly or supra-marginal advantages (goodwill) can be capitalised. The capital sum to which an annual income corresponds is calculated by dividing the annual income by the current rate of interest on pure Waiting and multiplying by a factor representing the certainty of the income. With the development of an organised market for securities, title-deeds to all kinds of income-yielding property—land and natural materials, shares in industrial enterprises, loans to joint-stock companies and to public bodies—all become mutually convertible: their individual peculiarities are submerged in their common characteristic of titles to income. The income derived from them—whether Rent, Interest, Profit or Net Monopoly-revenue—becomes merged in the general category of Income from Property.

Under modern institutions of private property and of an open market for securities, all incomes involving Institutional Revenue can be so capitalised. They then become title deeds of a perpetual claim upon the social product. Whatever their origin they are mutually convertible, and become merged in the general type of income-bearing Property.

The element of Institutional Revenue in personal activity is a permanent source of income similar to the return from land or material capital. The institutional restriction of opportunity that gives rise to it may persist while the individuals that perform the functions change. An individual occupying such a position of economic advantage may cease to perform the function, but by hiring the services of another person who enjoys no institutional privilege he may continue to draw Institutional Revenue. Examples are the profits of jurisdiction of a seigneur who appoints a deputy, the profits obtained by farming a state monopoly or the income enjoyed by a retired business man from the sale of 'goodwill'. Such sources of income can be capitalised and exchanged for incomes derived from ownership of land or material capital. Thus Institutional Revenue in incomes derived from personal effort may give rise to new forms of Property, interchangeable with and economically equivalent to property in physical goods. Examples of such property in the past are to be found in the commutation of feudal dues for single payments; the vendibility of offices under the *ancien régime* and the sale of commissions in the army in England before 1873; and transferable membership rights in privileged gilds or trading companies. In our own day such property is exemplified by bonus shares issued to shareholders in a joint-stock company in order to capitalise abnormal profits, the result either of exceptional opportunities or of organised monopoly; fully paid-up ordinary shares issued by a joint-stock company in payment of patent rights sold by a patentee; the purchase-price of a doctor's or a solicitor's practice; the capitalised value of membership of a bourse or stock-exchange.

24. *Work-incomes and Property-incomes.*—The distinction between incomes derived from Work and those derived from Property has been drawn and emphasised in recent economic theory, notably by Professor Cannan,[1] and Dr. Dalton.[2] Among the important differences between Work-incomes and Property-incomes is the fact that, while the ability to earn an income by work is a quality physically inherent in a man—a function of his bones and muscles, of his brain and senses—the right to income from property is merely attached to an individual by virtue of a social convention; it is a socially recognised claim, transferable and independent of the owner. Speaking generally, Property-incomes can be transferred by sale, gift or bequest; Work-incomes cannot. A work-income ceases with the physical or intellectual powers of its recipient; when he dies, it dies. A property-income may continue through an indefinite number of human generations; it continues to be paid if its recipient is infant or aged, imbecile or impotent, even if he is at the moment undiscoverable. From the distinction between Work-incomes and Property-incomes flow two consequences, both of which tend to narrow the circle of receivers of Institutional Revenue.

25. The first is the effect of the institution of Inheritance. In a very special and limited sense Work-incomes can be inherited, and this in two ways. First, inborn personal characteristics can be inherited; second, parents can

[1] *The Economic Outlook*, ch. i and vii; *Wealth*, ch. ix; *Review of Economic Theory*, ch. x–xiii.
[2] *The Inequality of Incomes*, Part III, ch. iii.

create for their children an evironment that promotes the development of capacity (i.e. can educate them in the broadest sense of the word). As to genetic inheritance, however, little is known with certainty (see p. 153). Environmental inheritance depends on institutions such as Property, Inheritance of Property and Education, so that the effect of such inheritance must be ascribed rather to these institutions than to any heritability of Work-incomes as such. Moreover, in the cases of both genetic and environmental inheritance active co-operation is required on the part of the inheritor. Unlike one who inherits legal claims, he must work, whatever talents or educational opportunities he may enjoy through being his parents' child.

But Property-incomes are directly inheritable and, in a community that permits freedom of bequest, no inheritance need fail for lack of natural heirs. As soon as an individual has made a fortune for himself in any way, he can found a family. Primogeniture in the past and a differential birth-rate in more recent times keep low the number of persons among whom the wealth of the successful ancestor is to be shared. These persons usually marry among their like. Thus wealthy families tend to form exclusive and numerically limited circles. These are then able through their wealth to obtain superior educational opportunities, special advantages in entering business, predominant influence in making lucrative appointments, and a disproportionate measure of political power, all of which things enable them to acquire fresh sources of Institutional Revenue for themselves. The influence of the Inheritance of Property in keeping Property-incomes within a few hands and in producing small classes of hereditarily wealthy persons has been commented on more often and more closely than that of any other institution.[1]

[1] For a good recent study of this subject see *The Economics of Inheritance* by J. Wedgwood.

26. The second consequence of this distinction between
Property-incomes and Work-incomes is one that to the
writer's knowledge has not so far been pointed out. It is
that, while one who relies on personal exertions for his
livelihood finds, after a certain point, increasing difficulty
in increasing his output of efficiency-units, one whose
income is due to legal claims is able, owing to the diminishing marginal utility of income, to increase the number of
those claims the more easily the more he already has. If a
man who relies on Work for his livelihood tries to increase
his income by putting forth more efficiency units of his
particular kind of work, he will find that after a certain
point it is increasingly difficult to earn more. An engineer
on piece-rates or a free-lance journalist, for instance,
may be able, by improving his efficiency or by intensifying
his exertions, to add 20 per cent. to his income; to add
40 per cent. will require more than proportionate effort;
while to add 60 per cent. will perhaps be the limit of his
powers. Even men of uncommon abilities who rise very
high in the scale of earnings reach the point after which
it is increasingly difficult to add to income.

On the other hand, an investor who by thrift and
prudence has increased his income by 20 per cent. will
find the effort of adding another 20 per cent. proportionately less, and so on with each successive increment
of 20 per cent. (This needs to be qualified by saying that
if an individual's supply of some factor, such as saving,
becomes commensurate with the world's total supply of
the factor, then the tendency to progressive ease of aug-
menting income will be counteracted by the tendency,
due to the law of diminishing returns, of further increases
in supply to lower the marginal net product of the factor
in all its applications. But individual incomes even of
multi-millionaires, have scarcely reached this point yet.)
This may be summarised by saying: incomes derived from

Work are increased with progressive difficulty, whereas those derived from Property are increased with regressive difficulty (progressive ease). In the building up of an individual fortune, as in many other things, it is the first steps that are the hardest. Every advantage gained in the form of acquisition of additional Property renders the remaining part of the task progressively lighter. In the case of incomes from Property it is true that money breeds money. It is a cumulative tendency. Taussig[1] summarises the causes of inequality as first, inborn differences in gifts; and second, the maintenance of unequal advantages through environment and through the inheritance of property. From the foregoing it will be seen that these two causes operate with unequal intensity, the second being cumulative in a way that the first is not.

Of course, the recipient of an income from Work may save out of it and thus enter the ranks of the Property-owners. But in this case his extra income is a Property-income. His Work-income as such soon reaches the 'ceiling' determined by his personal abilities and opportunities. Hence it follows that Property-incomes tend to contribute much more than Work-incomes to the inequality of wealth in modern communities.

27. We thus see that under any social system admitting free transference of such titles to income (such as a system based on freedom of enterprise and private property in instruments of production) there is an inherent tendency towards increasing inequality in incomes, which will be more pronounced if free disposal in bequest is also admitted. Catastrophic inflation of currency, unwise business speculation, or extravagant spending by the idle rich may dissipate great accumulations of wealth, but a cumulative force is perpetually operating, in any individualistic

[1] *Principles of Economics*, ch. lv, § 5.

society, which tends to make the rich richer and the poor at least relatively poorer. This tendency cannot be entirely counteracted by any extension of opportunities in the way of educational and credit facilities. It can only be counteracted, if at all, by very steeply graduated direct taxation on personal income and on inherited wealth. The justification of such taxation is, indeed, less on grounds of equity or convenience than on grounds of the desirability of checking inequality in income. A limit is reached when such taxation is carried so far as to impair the accumulation and use of wealth for productive purposes; that is, to endanger one of the fundamental institutions of the system concerned. In such a case we must say that inequality of wealth is inherent in the social system.

Examples are not far to seek of this tendency, inherent in any form of economic organisation based on private property, towards increasing inequality of income. The community of free, roughly equal, property-owning peasants, beloved of the distributivist writers, is inherently unstable and tends always to produce types such as the Grossbauer, the gombeen-man, the kulak—peasants who by labour, prudence, cunning or luck have acquired more land than their neighbours and who then either rent surplus land to their poorer neighbours, employ them for a wage, lend them stock or money at usurious rates of interest, or undertake the marketing of their produce at a monopolistic rate of profit. The history of the gild merchant and of the craft gild, of the regulated company and of the unregulated small master shows the same tendency; everywhere, in spite of organisation and regulations designed to maintain equality, not only of opportunity but of actual conditions, a society composed of numerous small producers, with little difference in wealth, each owning the tools of his trade and selling his own product direct to the consumer, gives way to a society differentiated into a few rich and many poor. This takes place through a division of function either between merchant and manufacturer-artisan, or between large master and small master working on commission, or between large master and journeyman working for wages. In any case the process of differentiation and division of function is accompanied by a concentration of property and a monopolisation of superior economic opportunities in the hands of the smaller and richer class.[1] In modern times, again, the tendency to the concentration of capital is undoubted. The proportion of small firms may, as some writers assert, remain unchanged or even increase; but the proportion of output controlled by large firms is constantly growing in all developed countries. Moreover, the independence of small firms is often illusory; the development of trade associations and cartels, the growth of the power of banks in industry, the practice of large firms maintaining small ones in a dependent position, practically working for them on commission, all these tendencies cause the concentration of real control to be greater than the concentration of nominal ownership as revealed by industrial statistics.[2]

28. The above considerations suggest a division into two classes of the objects of property. There is the social recognition and protection that confirms the individual in the possession on the one hand of concrete objects of enjoyment or of rights over them, and on the other hand of claims on society for income. This corresponds approximately to the distinction between property in means of consumption and in means of production, since the claims

[1] See G. Unwin, *Industrial Organisation in the Sixteenth and Seventeenth Centuries*.

[2] See J. A. Hobson, *Evolution of Modern Capitalism*; R. W. Liefmann, *Kartelle, Kouzerne und Trusts*; R. Hilferding, *Finance Capital*; N. Lenin, *Imperialism*.

referred to, though not themselves means of production, are based upon the ownership of such, coupled with the organisation of society on lines that gives a wide scope for enterprise with them. It is only to the former class of property objects that the psychological justification of property as a satisfaction of certain alleged inborn needs applies. Hence it may be possible that many of the abuses of present-day society could be removed by the modification or abolition of the latter class of property-objects without affecting the former. A limitation of the scope of property and of inheritance with respect to means of production would do much more to diminish inequality of individual income than taxation of large incomes after they have been received.

29. *Rent of Ability.*—One category of income has not yet been considered, namely, rent of ability, in the sense of the return to special personal qualities that cannot be produced by training and that happen to have high economic value. Thus the income of a Charlie Chaplin or an Edison, of a Caruso or a Bernard Shaw is mostly Rent of Ability. Rent of Ability is part of the general category of Work-income. Being dependent on personal qualities it cannot be transferred to others, nor does it survive the recipient. It is true that Rent of Ability is a surplus akin to rent, because it is the return to a restricted factor, but since the restriction is not due to any particular social institutions it is not Institutional Revenue. However, since it can be used for the purchase of titles to perpetual and transferable Property-income, it may give rise to Institutional Revenue. Rent of Ability does not include the earnings of the ordinarily competent professional or business man, since the supply of such can be increased by appropriate training and is responsive to changes in the wage offered. In so far as their earnings are above the average this is due to Institutional Restriction of their supply and the surplus must be reckoned as Institutional Revenue.

30. *Conjuncture-gains.*—There is yet another category of income, first pointed out by German economists under the name of conjuncture-gains (Konjunktur-Gewinne).[1] By conjuncture is meant the whole of the economic situation at a given moment: the state of technique, of fashion, of the market; it includes the vicissitudes of the trade-cycle—depression or exaltation—as well as less regular movements of trade, such as those due to new inventions or to war, or famine and pestilence. Conjuncture-gains are then the unearned increment that accrues to an economic subject through unforeseen changes in the economic situation. Examples are war profits and rises in land-values. In the writer's opinion, much opportunity income, like quasi-rent, disappears if it be considered in a sufficiently long run. Most of the apparent windfalls in trade, especially those due to the normal trade-cycle, occur with enough regularity over a long period to have a statistical average value: this must influence the supply of entrants to that branch of trade. In other words, these particular chances are discounted in advance, roughly it is true, but effectively. However, in a progressive society there will be a permanent surplus of positive Conjuncture-gains. This kind of income is to be classified as Institutional Revenue, or not, according to the circumstances which give rise to it and the form of its appropriation. If certain social institutions create the necessity of providing against the uncertainty of a particular conjunctural opportunity-charge and if this provision is a source of income to some person or persons, then a further source of Institutional

---

[1] It is the same element in income that J. B. Clark calls 'Profit'. According to him it emerges only in the dynamic state. (*Distribution of Wealth.*)

Revenue may be present. For instance, the vagaries of fashion or the movements of speculative markets create a part of the normal income of the business man, whose services could be obtained more cheaply were these smoothed out. Income obtained from a rise in land-values, although due to a change in the economic opportunity, is purely an institutional creation, and is entirely Institutional Revenue. On the other hand some income ascribed to mere opportunity may be due in reality to personal qualities, such as intuition, instinctive foresight, or that 'flair' for a situation that makes a successful man of affairs. In this case it is properly Rent of Ability. There remain, however, a certain number of cases of income due to pure chance, such as those made out of wars or those made out of conditions created by new inventions made by other people. These are conjuncture-incomes in the narrow sense. They have played an important part in the process of accumulation of capital, on which so much industrial progress has depended. They fall as a perquisite to whatever class occupies a strategical position in the organisation of the community. Under modern conditions they are appropriated as a rule by the landowner or by the business man. In so far as institutional restrictions form the basis of such appropriation, they must be classified as Institutional Revenue.

Conjuncture-gains that involve no element of Institutional Revenue we may call Pure Conjuncture-gains. These fall to the lot of certain individuals whose services or whose property happen to be in demand. Like Rent of Ability, Pure Conjuncture Gains are a surplus determined entirely by demand. We may therefore group these species of income together as Personal Rent.

31. *Basic Earnings.*—A title is needed for income that does not fall under the above categories. It corresponds to the

earnings of Labour of normal ability in non-restricted trades, plus whatever part of the return to Waiting and Uncertainty-bearing is not due to Institutional Restriction. Let it be called Basic Earnings.

32. In this way we get a classification of forms of income that cuts across the traditional one of Wages, Profits, Interest and Rent with a new division into Basic Earnings, Personal Rent and Institutional Revenue. These two bases of classification correspond to two different points of view, to economic statics and to economic dynamics. To consider income as the return to various factors of production is convenient for the analysis of Marshall's stationary state; to consider it as determined by social institutions in its division between certain groups is convenient for many discussions in sociology and economic history.

Large individual incomes may be due either to Personal Rent or to Institutional Revenue, but their social significance is very different in the two cases. Personal Rent is due to causes peculiar to the individual—a favourable combination of individual aptitudes or resources and of the community's effective demand. Institutional Revenue is due to the working of social institutions and consequently affects definite social categories of persons. Also it tends to perpetuate itself and it becomes interwoven with other social phenomena, whereas large incomes of the former class tend to be isolated events. In other words, Personal Rent need not while Institutional Revenue must be the basis for the development of economic classes.

THE STATISTICAL EVIDENCE FOR THE EXISTENCE OF NON-COMPETING GROUPS WITHIN THE COMMUNITY

WE will consider here four studies on the subject of non-competing groups. These are an article by Sir Sydney Chapman and Mr. Marquis on the recruitment of employers in the cotton industry,[1] books by Mr. Llewellyn Lewis[2] and Mr. Kenneth Lindsay[3] on the after-careers of ex-elementary school children, and an article by Mr. Ginsberg on interchange between social classes.[4]

Sir Sydney Chapman estimated by means of general inquiries and by means of a questionnaire issued to employers in the cotton industry chosen at random, the proportion of employers and managers that began life as wage-earners. His results refer to the two chief branches of the industry, manufacturing and spinning, and are as follows, showing percentage of first-generation employers to total number:—

Manufacturing:—   *Per cent.*
   By questionnaire (79 per cent of those addressed replied) .. 76
   By general inquiry   63

Spinning:—

	Per cent.
By questionnaire (69 per cent. replied) { managing directors..	73
managers	84
By general inquiry .. .. { managing directors..	13
managers	42
assistant managers ..	67

The method adopted is open to many objections, some of which were brought out in the discussion that followed the

[1] S. J. Chapman and F. J. Marquis, 'The Recruiting of the Employing Classes from the Ranks of the Wage-Earners in the Cotton Industry', *J.R.Stat.Soc.*, LXXV, February 1912, p. 293.
[2] E. Llewellyn Lewis, *The Children of the Unskilled*, 1924.
[3] K. Lindsay, *Social Progress and Educational Waste*, 1926.
[4] M. Ginsberg, 'Interchange Between Social Classes', *Economic Journal*, December 1929, XXXIX, p. 554.

paper: certainly the fact that the figures given by general inquiry, covering a much greater number of cases, are uniformly lower than those given by the questionnaire is significant. Also, the industry selected was, at the time that the paper was written, a peculiarly favourable one as regards mobility. It was keenly competitive, monopoly had little scope in it, external economies were many and accessible, experience was easily obtained in minor supervising posts, credit was cheap and easily obtained. It is known that the capable poor man's opportunities for advancement were greater in it than in most other industries. Sir Sydney Chapman has not extended his investigations to the engineering and ship-building, to the iron and steel, to the non-ferrous metal or to the chemical industries. In the absence of definite data it is unsafe to dogmatise, but few would expect to find in these industries such a high proportion of employers recruited from the ranks of workers. Again, Sir Sydney Chapman's method of approach is not the best. Instead of considering the proportion of employers recruited from among wage-earners we should rather consider the proportion of wage-earners who rise to managerial positions. Given complete mobility we should expect the employing class to be recruited from wage-earners in about the same proportion that wage-earners bear to the total number of persons engaged in the industry.[1] What do we find? We find that at the most

---

[1] Although not directly germane to the present discussion it is worth while pointing out an error in Sir Sydney Chapman's mathematical analysis of the long-period effect on the national dividend of an increase in the number of employers. In it there occurs the expression:

$$\frac{P' - P}{K} = f(c) - \left\{ \frac{\partial p}{\partial c}c + \frac{\partial p}{\partial l}l \right\} + \frac{P}{E}(E + K)$$

where P = national product when no. of employers = E
       P′ = national product when no. of employers increases to
            E + K
       p = product of one firm = $f(c)$
       c = capital (including land) in one firm
       l = labour employed in one firm.

Since $\frac{\partial p}{\partial c}c - \frac{\partial p}{\partial l}l$ are the employer's expenses and since they must favourable estimate, the wage-earners supply 73 to 84 per cent. of the managers and directors while, according to the Census of 1911, in the Lancashire cotton industry wage-earners form 99·65 per cent. of the total, or 99·11 per cent. if one only counts male workers. A more direct approach to the subject would be an investigation of the proportion in which positions in my groups (1) and (2) are filled from persons in groups (4) and (5) compared with the proportion the two latter groups bear to the whole population. Since a particular type of calculation is correlated with a particular group, this question would be almost answered by an analysis of the after-careers of elementary school-children with respect to the position that they ultimately attain.

This has been done in the two books referred to. *The Children of the Unskilled* is a review of 450 families, containing 2,000 children of elementary school age, taken from Glasgow, Middlesbrough, and Blaenau Festiniog (N. Wales). Out of 13,930 children leaving school each year it was estimated that about 1,330 are apprenticed to skilled trades, that is about 9·5 per cent. The better-off families are able to apprentice a greater proportionate number of children than the poorer ones. Economic pressure forces the children (especially the eldest child) of an unskilled worker to enter unskilled work at the earliest possible age in order to help support the family.

Social Progress and Educational Waste is a study of the scholarship system and of scholars' after-careers in the whole of England and Wales, with special reference to London, Oxfordshire, Bradford, Warrington and Wallasey. Out of

be less than $f(c)$ if the marginal employer is to get any remuneration at all for the work that he does, it is shown that an increase in the number of employers will increase the national dividend.

However, the sign of the last term is wrong; the expression should read:

$$\frac{P' - P}{K} = f(c) - \left\{\frac{\partial p}{\partial c}c + \frac{\partial p}{\partial l}l\right\} - \frac{P}{E}(E + K)$$

leaving indeterminate the question whether an increase in the number of employers would increase the national dividend.

550,000 children who leave elementary schools each year, approximately 9·5 per cent. proceed to secondary schools, while 1 per 1,000 reach the University. Of 2,800,000 adolescents, 80 per cent. are not in full-time attendance at any school. Yet evidence is brought forward in this book that at least 50 per cent. of the pupils in elementary schools can benefit by some form of post-primary education up to the age of sixteen. Under 10 per cent. of the jobs done by ex-elementary-school leavers can be described as skilled work. Yet when we come to consider the secondary-school pupils, we find that, while only 6 per cent. of them are children of unskilled workers and only 26 per cent. can be described as of working-class origin, 58 per cent. of ex-secondary-school leavers go on to further education or enter directly into professional, clerical or commercial occupations.

Finally Mr. Ginsberg's article on 'Interchange between Social Classes' contains an analysis of the occupations of 3,775 individuals belonging to the present generation and of those of their parents and grandparents. According to occupation the subjects of the investigation are divided into three classes:

Class I includes professionals, employers I, own account I.
Class II includes employers II, own account II, salaried officials, elementary school teachers.
Class III includes wage-earners, skilled, semi-skilled, and unskilled.

Considering only the present generation and their fathers the following results emerge:—

TABLE I

Comparison of the occupations of the present generation with those of their fathers (percentage of present generation).

			PRESENT GENERATION		
			Class I	Class II	Class III
FATHERS	Class I	..	33·0	7·0	0·69
	Class II	..	54·9	52·7	27·1
	Class III	..	11·9	40·2	72·3

Movements from class to class may be summarised as follows
(figures as percentages of present generation):—

Upward Movement

From III to I	From II to I	From III to II
12	55	40

Downward Movement

From I to III	From I to II	From II to III
0·6	7	27

Remaining in Own Class

Class I	Class II	Class III
33	52	72

(Discrepancies between these figures and those in Table I are
Mr. Ginsberg's.)

The figures for grandfathers indicate greater downward
mobility but less upward mobility during the previous
generation.

The general conclusion to be drawn from these figures and
from others published by Mr. Ginsberg in the same article,
referring to admissions to Lincoln's Inn, and to Professor
Bowley's investigations into social conditions of the working-
class population of certain towns, is that mobility between
social classes, although increasing, is at present small.

CHAPTER VI

SOME CRITICISMS OF THE THEORY OF INSTITUTIONAL REVENUE

In this chapter we shall deal with some criticisms of the theory of Institutional Revenue that has been developed in the preceding part of the work. The first two are based on purely verbal misunderstandings. The third is more fundamental.

1. The use of the term Institutional Revenue is perhaps likely to give rise to a misconception, namely, that some income is in itself institutional in contradistinction to some other income that is natural. It is not intended to imply this. In the writer's opinion all income is institutional in the sense that it is only through social institutions that any income at all can be either produced or enjoyed. The special phrase Institutional Revenue is used to denote that part of an individual's income that is due to an Institutional Restriction of some factor of production supplied by him. An income guaranteed by an institution that involves no restriction is not Institutional Revenue. All income is institutional but not all is Institutional Revenue in the sense of the definition. Thus, the payment of wages to an unskilled labourer or the earning of income by a self-employed capital-less workman depends on social institutions. Such wages or earnings are, in this sense, an institutional income. But if no Institutional Restriction of the labourer's services exists, his income involves no Institutional Revenue.

2. This misconception has its converse in another criticism of the conception of Institutional Revenue. This is that

all income is not only institutional but involves Institutional Revenue since every institution, being a regulation of human activity, involves a restriction. If, for instance, the institution of private property restricts the activity of individuals with regard to the provision of certain factors of production, so in a different way does that of public property; for the greater the scope of public property the less becomes that of private property and the freedom of individual enterprise is thereby lessened. But this objection is based on a verbal confusion. The word restriction is used by the critic first in the sense of the inhibition of human efforts effected in some direction or other by all institutions and is used afterwards in the special technical sense here given to it. All institutions imply the regulation of human activity but all regulations of human activity are not of such a sort as to involve Restriction of the supply of a factor of production.

3. Let us now examine another and much more searching criticism of the theory implied in the following question. The whole conception of Institutional Restriction and Revenue contains the implicit assumption of a social system involving no Institutional Restriction, with which the existing system is compared. What, then, is the hypothetical standard with which existing income-distribution is compared?

The answer to this question is that in effect the hypothetical basis of comparison is either the ideal individualistic society or the ideal communistic society. For in this case extremes certainly do meet and the logical conclusion of either individualism or communism is substantially the same form of social organisation. The central idea of individualism, when translated into economic categories, is equality of opportunity. To this end liberalism has sought the abolition of legal and political inequalities, has established the reign of law and the watch-dog state. But to achieve true equality of opportunity it would have to go further and abolish inheritance and private property in means of acquisition, since, as has been shown, these institutions provide a spring-board from which a man can jump off ahead of his fellows. The central idea of communism is the achievement of a class-less society, that is, one in which no class-monopoly of power or wealth should exist. This end it seeks through existing technical administrative and social developments (for example: the growing size of the industrial unit and the tendency towards planned production, the increasing importance of the non-owning technical expert, the rising class-consciousness and more powerful organisation of the working class). Socialism, i.e., the public ownership of means of production, is not for the communist an end in itself, but a means to the end: the establishment of an equalitarian society. Individualism emphasises the destructive sides: the abolition of institutions that obstruct equality of opportunity, while communism stresses the constructive side: evolving out of existing material the institutions that would guarantee equality of opportunity.

By definition, Restriction resides in any conditions affecting supply that tend to raise the marginal net product of the factor supplied. But by a train of argument common to all economists from the classical economists to the author of *The Economics of Welfare* it is shown that that which tends to increase equality of opportunity in the supply of a restricted factor tends also to lower that factor's marginal productivity and to raise that of all other factors. Hence Inequality of Opportunity and Institutional Restriction have the same connotation. In spite of this the term Institutional Restriction will be retained: partly because it suggests the social mechanism and the effects on distribution of Inequality of Opportunity better than that somewhat colourless and negative term, and partly because that term has come to acquire, through being bandied about in popular discussion, such an indefinite and far from precise meaning that it could well be banished from the economic vocabulary.[1]

Institutions which promote equality of opportunity diminish Institutional Restriction and thus create less Institutional Revenue. Our hypothetical social system embodying complete equality of opportunity would be one giving rise to no Institutional Revenue. This must be understood as a mental construction, introduced for the purpose of analysis and to make explicit what was from the first implicit. It is analogous to Wieser's ideal communistic society in which all goods would exchange for their real values,[2] used similarly as a schema or mental construction.

[1] R. T. Ely connects the idea of Inequality of Opportunity with that of surplus-value. He distinguishes (*Property and Contract*, ch. xvi) four different kinds of economic surplus, viz.: (1) 'a gain over and above such a return to the owners of factors of production as will induce them to play their part in the work of production' (Hobson's surplus); (2) 'a surplus over and above something received by a non-privileged class' (the present writer's Institutional Revenue); (3) 'a surplus over and above general subsistence'; (4) 'the wealth produced by the worker over and above what he receives' (Marx's surplus-value). This first kind ('economic surplus in the narrow sense') he divides into five parts, viz.: (1) rent of land; (2) interest on supra-marginal saving; (3) net monopoly-revenue; (4) conjuncture gains; (5) personal surplus (rent of ability). Referring to the second kind of surplus he points out that the movement in favour of equality of opportunity has usually taken the form of an attack on privilege. In the early days of American history it was aimed at political privilege and took the form of a demand for political equality. Later it turned against economic privilege and obtained free land, free schools, etc., but it soon found sharp limitations to its further progress in the shape of the institutions of property, inheritance, contract, and other vested rights.

[2] F. von Wieser, *Natural Value*, Bk. II, ch. vi and Bk. VI, ch. v.

CHAPTER VII

SOME APPLICATIONS OF THE THEORY OF INSTITUTIONAL REVENUE

The reader who has persevered so far with the analysis here presented of the various categories of income will probably feel inclined to ask: What next? To what does this all lead? Although the purpose of this book is rather to forge a tool than to use it, nevertheless the fashioner of an implement may reasonably be expected, if only in justification of the time and labour spent on it, to bring forward some indications of its possible employment.

Three applications of the theory of Institutional Revenue will be suggested here; one historical, one critical, and one practical or political.

1. The first application of the theory of Institutional Revenue is to sociology and to the philosophy of history.

It is not suggested that the incidence of Institutional Revenue is merely arbitrary. Every social system, every stage of economic development is characterised by certain methods of production and of organisation of production. For their proper unfolding and working these require certain social institutions. These institutions involve the restriction of certain factors to certain groups and hence the occurrence of certain forms of Institutional Revenue. For example, feudalism was embodied in the institutions of the manor, of homage and of private jurisdiction. These involved a ruling military hierarchy and the payment of feudal dues and labour-rents. The *ancien régime* was embodied in the institutions of the absolute state, of orders and their privileges, of landownership and of gild-organisation. These involved rents and *banalités*, tithes, sinecures, profits of privileged merchants and master-craftsmen. Capitalism is embodied in the institutions of private property in the means of production, free enterprise, and enforcement of contract. These necessarily imply the existence of a class of capitalist entrepreneurs and rentiers and the payment of rent, royalties, interest and profit.

There is thus the possibility of using the concept of Institutional Revenue as an engine of analysis in historical or sociological study. Changes in social institutions involve changes in the composition of groups drawing Institutional Revenue from society and in the amount of the income so drawn. Owing to the close-knit nature of the social fabric, changes that appear to have no economic significance whatever may be intimately bound up with changes that have.

There are two extreme positions in the philosophy of history, the materialistic and the idealistic. The first holds that human events are determined by environmental factors, in the last analysis of the material order, geographical, climatic, technological and economic; and that the social environment, including political, religious and philosophical ideas, are the reflex in men's consciousness of these external causes. The opposite view holds that the external development, the mastery over nature and the development of culture are due to the internal factors, that fundamentally it is the consciousness and will of man that is ever moulding the world into a fuller harmony with the needs of his being. Without necessarily committing ourselves to the first view in its entirety, it is easy to see that in many cases economic factors have been of enormous importance in determining historical events. Not least among these factors have been struggles for power between rival sections of society with different economic foundations and consequently different and often opposing interests. Political movements frequently take the form of an attempt by one group to modify or abolish an Institutional Restriction enjoyed by another or to set up one for itself. One does not need to be a Marxian to realise the part played in social development by various forms of income-getting and the importance of vested interests and of the struggles that they give rise to as engines of social change.

Although the thesis of this book is logically distinct from the Marxian theory of society—no one who accepts the former is thereby committed to the holding of the latter—the concept of Institutional Revenue can be made to fit into the Marxian system very conveniently. There must be a considerable number of persons who are inclined to accept the Materialistic Conception of History and Sociology but who refuse to accept the Labour Theory of Value and the theory of Surplus Value which appears to be based on it. The concept of Institutional Revenue is one which, while it does not involve the fallacies of the labour theory of value, can play exactly the same part as Surplus-value in sociological and historical theory.

2. The second application of the theory is by way of criticism of current economic theory. The idea here put forward of the rôle of social institutions in economic life will, if accepted, make untenable the naïve conception that certain social institutions and the economic practices founded on them are 'natural' and that all other arrangements represent an 'artificial' interference with the natural order. It might be thought that this critical work is now fifty years out of date, were it not for the recrudescence in many academic circles, both in Great Britain and on the Continent, of the simple-minded outlook on social institutions of Ricardo and J. B. Clark. By drawing attention to the manner in which the determination of value and hence the distribution of income in the present form of society is affected by institutions of property, inheritance, contract and the like, the line of thought set forth in this book should tend to make it impossible to hold that there is anything particularly natural or normal about a society in which property rights are recognised in non-human instruments of production but not in human beings, in which some contracts are enforced but not others, in which the state forbids certain forms of acquisition (designated theft, fraud, or blackmail) but permits others (monopoly, usury, speculation in land values). *Laisser-faire* individualism is just as 'artificial' as mercantilism or collectivism. Each form of society is characterised by certain institutions: in each certain forms of distribution will 'naturally' arise as a consequence of these institutions. Change these and you modify the scheme of distribution.[1]

While criticising the attitude which regards a particular institutional system as enjoying a unique position in economic theory, the writer does not consider it any part of his intention to imply any ethical judgment by his concept of Institutional Revenue. Far from him be it to draw the conclusion that, because form of income involves Institutional Revenue, it 'ought' not to be appropriated by the group that does so, or that, because certain other

[1] 'One would have to be an idiot nowadays to deny the influence of socially created institutions and rules upon the distribution of wealth. . . . With this (marginal productivity) the theory of marginal value had only produced the incomplete torso of a theory of distribution, and was moreover quite conscious of this fact. It did not profess to exhaust the manifold developments of reality with this formula; on the contrary it was not slow to emphasise in repeated and explicit announcements, that to its previous researches must be added a second series of researches whose task should be to investigate just those alterations in the simple formula which were bound to be elicited by the introduction of new assumptions of a "social" nature.' (E. v. Böhm-Bawerk, *Macht oder ökonomisches Gesetz*, in his *Gesammelte Schriften*, pp. 230, 234.)

groups are receiving less than they would were certain Institutional Restrictions removed, they are obtaining less than the 'full product of their labour' and that they 'ought' therefore to be getting more. The scientific study of society, of which economics is a part, can admit only utilitarian criteria of good and can pronounce only objective judgments on social processes. The justice or injustice of any particular form of distribution, of any particular kind of Institutional Revenue depends on the expediency or inexpediency of the institutions of which they are the necessary corollary. On the other hand it is the writer's desire to point out the essentially institutional nature of distribution. The prevailing form of distribution is not more natural than others that are known to history. It depends on a complex of social institutions, just as they did. Moreover, it contains institutional restrictions just as real, although concealed under a formal equality of rights and opportunities, as they contained. Its 'justice' has been defended on the ground that every member of society does, on the whole, get the value of his contribution to the social product as measured by a strictly impartial and impersonal process in which social usefulness is the sole title to an imputation of value. This defence is at least as illegitimate as the accusation of 'injustice' based on the grounds quoted above. A great many possible social systems could exist, each involving various Institutional Restrictions in greater or less degree and each resulting in a special form of distribution; under each system every individual would be getting 'what he produced'. The social conditions of production being different, the share would be different, yet under all it would be possible to defend the resultant state of affairs as 'just'. All that can safely be predicted of any distributionary conditions is that they are in accordance with the social system under which they arise. To one born into and brought up under such a system its arrangements appear more 'natural' than those of any other and thus he takes them as the norm of judgment and comparison; to one who, in addition, belongs to one of the groups favoured by the system, its arrangements will appear not only 'natural' but also and on that account 'just'. These are, however, affective and not scientific judgments.

3. In the third place, the theory of Institutional Revenue has some bearing upon political and social policy. If the distribution of wealth is a function of social institutions then the activity of those persons whose aim is to effect a more equal distribution of wealth than that which prevails at present must be directed towards the conscious and deliberate re-casting of the institutions of Government, Property, Inheritance, Education, the Family, etc., in the light of their influence on distribution. A comparative study of institutions and their influence upon distribution suggests that the scheme of distribution that exists in a community at any given time is much more flexible than the practical man or the *laisser-faire* economist supposes, and that there is a considerable range of possible institutional frameworks within each of which 'natural' economic laws would work, producing different distributional effects.

Generally speaking inequality will tend to diminish the more instruments of production are public property rather than private property, the more inheritance is restricted, the greater is the mobility of labour, the greater is the equality of political rights enjoyed by members of the community, the more educational opportunities are independent of the means and social position of parents, and the less considerations of property influence marriage. Any change in the above-mentioned institutions must, however, be carefully scrutinised with a view to detecting undesired secondary reactions. Finally the fact must not be lost sight of that social institutions are not separate entities; the institutions of a given society cohere and form what is known as a social system. Before the reformer begins to tinker with single institutions he should try to envisage the social system as a whole and understand the interwovenness of its separate parts, of those that he wishes to preserve as well as those that he wishes to alter. If he desires to make extensive changes in the existing social structure he should endeavour to make for himself a picture of the state of affairs that he would like to bring about, not as a bundle of isolated institutions but as a correlated system.

Without venturing to outline in further detail any particular scheme of social reconstruction, the author would like to offer a few observations, which seem to follow directly from the concept of Institutional Revenue, upon such schemes in general. Since Institutional Revenue can arise out of a great variety of social institutions, it is unlikely that the entire blame for maldistribution is due to a single institution. Hence there is a *prima facie* case against projects like the Single Tax upon land-values, which proceeds upon the assumption that the private appropriation of land is solely responsible for distributive injustice. The same may be said of such ideas as that the reform of the credit system or the abolition of ordinary commercial and industrial monopoly would produce a state of greater equality. Economic rent and monopoly revenue are only species of a larger genus, to which all forms of income from property belong. The argument of sections 26 and 27 of Chapter V suggest that inequality is a necessary consequence of any form of private property in the means of production. Thus a certain scepticism is indicated towards prohibitions or special taxes that leave untouched the general fabric of institutions, and towards schemes of fiscal redistribution or of state control that aim at welding some of the external characteristics of socialism to a social order that is still fundamentally individualistic. Even the reformers who tilt at all forms of private property in the means of production are too limited in their scope. The restriction of educational opportunities, a gild system, or a caste-structure of society may enshrine forms of Institutional Revenue quite as productive of inequality as those resulting from the private ownership of land and capital.

Reformers who are concerned with objects other than the redistribution of wealth should consider whether their proposals may not have unexpected secondary effects on distribution. For example, any system of regulating entry into an occupation by registration or licensing may set up vested interests and give rise to Institutional Revenue. The generalisation of the privileges of incorporation and of limited liability has created a new form of property in industrial enterprise. The entry of women into callings hitherto reserved to men is producing unexpected effects upon the relative share of men and women in the social dividend.

SUMMARY

CHAPTER I

INTRODUCTORY

1. Inequality of wealth is an obvious social fact.

2. The plain man's three theories to account for inequality:—

    (1) chance,
    (2) personal qualities,
    (3) force or fraud.

The second and third contain elements of truth but are subject to obvious criticisms.

3. The economists' answers:—

    (1) The economist of the Historical School gives a descriptive account of social institutions affecting distribution of wealth.
    (2) The economist of the Analytical School gives an analysis of income into rent, interest, profit, and wages.

Neither gives a complete answer to the plain man's questions.

4. There are two ways in which economics and the study of social institutions can be of mutual service:—

    (1) The development of an economic interpretation of social forms.
    (2) A study of social institutions from the point of view of economic theory.

The second of these is all that is aimed at in this book. The method adopted is that of the Analytical School of Economics.

5. A brief review of tendencies in the study of Economics since 1848. The complacency of the post-classical school was disturbed by four influences:—

    (1) The rise of the German Historical School.
    (2) The Mathematical Economists.
    (3) The Austrian School.
    (4) The Socialists and the reaction against them.

The last three influences combined to form modern analytical economics. Economics became divided into two distinct sciences: economic history and abstract economics.

6. The present work is an attempt to combine the analytical method of the modern marginal school with the historical economists' recognition of the existence and influence of social institutions. It proposes to develop a theory of distribution which, while adhering strictly to the principle of marginal valuation, is capable of taking into account the part played by the social framework.

7. The main argument is divided into four parts:—
    (1) Discussion of Social Institutions;
    (2) Theory of Value; leading to
    (3) Theory of Factor-Distribution;
    (4) Theory of Personal Distribution.

CHAPTER II

DISCUSSION OF SOCIAL INSTITUTIONS

1. The word 'Institution' is used in two ways:—
    (a) a norm of social behaviour with regard to some function or functions;
    (b) an organisation in which this norm is embodied, or which preserves and maintains it.

2. (a) An Institution is based on a function or functions. A function is defined as a type of specific human activity. An institution is concerned with social behaviour; all persons living in a community partake in its institutions.

3. (b) Corresponding to some of these social norms there is an organisation, or organisations, of human beings. In other cases, the norm is embodied in no definite organisation, but exists in the shape of numerous individual acts, but these individual acts occur within a social framework.
    In this work the word Institution is used in sense (a).

4. An empirical classification of Institutions is into:—
    1. Economic Organisation.
        Economic Organisation in ⎰(a) Labour Organisation;
        the narrower sense   ⎱(b) Organisation of Enterprise;
                                  (c) Political Organisation.

  2. Property (including Inheritance and Contract).
  3. Status :—

    (*a*) Class;
    (*b*) Order;
    (*c*) Caste.

  4. The Family (including Marriage).
  5. Education.
  6. Religion.

5. Social Institutions are interconnected and interdependent: they form a correlated whole. The complex of all social institutions is a social system.

6. 1. *Economic Organisation.*—Economic activity is social activity. Therefore economic organisation is a form of social organisation, and involves a framework of social institutions. Reasons for including Political Organisation.

7. (*a*) *Labour Organisation.*—The chief forms of organisation of labour are :—

    (i) Independent Labour;
    (ii) Wage Labour;
    (iii) Serfdom;
    (iv) Slavery.

Under all these forms, associations of workers or bodies representative of workers may exercise certain functions, such as the regulation and control of conditions of work and the protection of the labourer's interest in the sale of his products or of his labour.

8. (*b*) *Organisation of Enterprise.*—Enterprise involves the union of business organisation with the use of capital.

9. Business organisation means the initiation and control of production, and the choice of methods of production.

10. Capital, that is to say produced means of production, depends on two things: (i) saving, or postponement of consumption, which directs productive power into the making of instrumental goods rather than consumption goods, and (ii) the organisation that directs this productive power so as to produce the material forms of capital that are needed. The latter is what is called here the organisation of capital.

11. Organisation of capital and business organisation are closely connected, since control over economic processes cannot be divided from control over the means whereby they are achieved. The combination of the two is called Enterprise.

12. The Organisation of Enterprise may take the following forms:—

   1. Private Enterprise—

      (a) Individual enterprise.

      (b) Associative enterprise—

         α. Associations of capital-owners.

         β. Associations of workers.

         γ. Associations of consumers.

   2. Public Enterprise.

(Public enterprise is essentially associative: it is also called Collective Enterprise.) There are forms of enterprise intermediate between 1 (b) and 2.

13. Corresponding to these forms of Enterprise occur various forms of Property, but there is no exact correlation of, say, public enterprise to public property.

14. Important among specific instances of the organisation of enterprise are the undertakings and organisations which together form the credit-system. Essentially concerned with the supply of capital, this system has acquired two other functions: (a) control over industry, (b) the creation of money.

15. (c) *Political Organisation.*—Political Organisation is the inclusive and compulsory organisation of the community as a whole for the preservation of the other institutions that make up the social system. Its function is general organisation and administration; it is concerned not so much with particular economic activities as with the general regulation of economic activity. Its functions include the acquisition of the means whereby it exists. The typical form is the State, although the State may come to exercise other functions, such as the organisation of labour and of enterprise.

16. 2. *Property.*—Property is defined as 'the exclusive right to control an economic good'. (R. T. Ely.)

   Property rights may be classified:—

I. According to the owning subject—

II. According to the owned object—

      (a) Intensively.

      (b) Extensively.

17. I. According to the owning subject—

    (1) Private Property:—

        (*a*) Individual.
        (*b*) Associative.

    (2) Public Property (essentially Associative or Collective).

18. II. A. In intensiveness, according to the nature of the thing owned.

    (1) Consumption Goods—

        (*a*) durable,
        (*b*) non-durable.

    (2) Production Goods—

        1. Labour—

            (*a*) the person of the labourer,
            (*b*) the services of the labourer.

        2. Capital Goods—

            (*a*) durable (fixed capital),
            (*b*) non-durable (circulating capital).

        3. Land.

19. II. B. In extensiveness, according to the extent of control exercised over the economic good.

    (1) Property rights may inhere in several different uses of the same object and the rights to different uses may be vested in so many different owners. (E.g. the rights of owner and tenant in a house; of shareholder and debenture-holder in a company.)

    (2) Property-rights may be limited as to particular uses, as when destruction or alienation of the object is prohibited.

    (3) Property-rights may be limited by conditions imposed by public authority, such as Factory Acts or the regulation of Public Utilities.

    (4) The exercise of property-rights may be limited in time, as in the case of patents and copyright.

20. *Inheritance.*—Restrictions on the right of disposal of one's property after one's death are even commoner than restrictions on the use of it during one's life. Only highly individualistic communities permit free testamentary disposition. The community usually limits Inheritance more than it limits Property. Examples are the institution of the legitim, the law of mortmain, legacy and succession duties, and the interference of the State with charitable bequests and trusts.

21. The objects of Inheritance are threefold:—

  (1) The preservation of the system of private property.
  (2) The provision of a motive for accumulation.
  (3) The well-being of the family.

22. *Contract.*—Contract is defined as 'an agreement of economic significance which is enforceable by public authority' (R. T. Ely). From the economic point of view there is no essential distinction between property rights and contract rights. The latter can be classified in exactly the same way as the former. Society is, however, usually more ready to limit contract rights on grounds of public utility than it is to limit the rights of property.

23. Effects of the Institution of Property (including Inheritance and Contract) on the distribution of wealth.

  1. With regard to the Subject of Ownership, the relative extension of private property and public property affects the distribution of income. Private property favours inequality (see Chapter V, sections 26–27); public property may favour equality.
  2. With regard to the Object of Ownership,

    A. intensively, the recognition or non-recognition of property-rights in human beings and in instruments of production has far-reaching effects;
    B. extensively, the imposition of conditions on ownership and contract is a potent method of social regulation of income.

24. 3. *Status.*—Under this head are grouped a number of institutions concerned with personal freedom and unfreedom.

25. Freedom may be classified as—

  A. Freedom of Thought,
  B. Freedom of Action:
    1. Political Freedom—
      (*a*) passive;
      (*b*) active.

    2. Economic Freedom.

26. A. Freedom of Thought has no direct, but much indirect, influence upon economic life.

27. B. 1. Passive political freedom means the secure enjoyment of civil rights. Active political freedom means a share in sovereignty. Liberty necessarily involves equality, in the sense of equality of rights. Political freedom tends to be used as a means to economic freedom.

28. B. 2. Economic freedom is the freedom to choose an occupation and follow it without special restrictions. Economic liberty involves equality of opportunity. Exclusion of certain categories of persons from the following of particular occupations tends to diminish the economic value of the labour of those persons. Economic liberty and equality of economic opportunity tend to maximise social well-being.

29. Economic freedom is impaired under certain institutions, of which the chief are Class, Order and Caste.

30. (a) *Class.*—Economic classes are groups differentiated according to income and economic opportunity, but not rigidly separated. They form non-competing groups. There may be some mobility between classes and class distinctions may co-exist with political equality.

31. (b) *Order.*—Orders are groups whose inequality of status is formally established by positive law or custom having the force of law. An individual's social and political rights and duties depend on his Order. Membership is usually hereditary, but it is sometimes possible for individuals to change from one Order to another. One example of this kind of status is that of serfdom.

32. Slavery is the lowest status in a system of Orders and is the most complete negation of freedom. There are variations in the extension of the slave owner's rights permitted under the slavery codes of different communities.

33. (c) *Caste.*—Castes are hereditary occupational groups. Distinctions based on birth and occupation easily develop into distinctions of wealth, owing to monopoly of certain occupations enjoyed by each caste.

34. Closely allied to caste-distinctions are those based on racial inequality. Races may form non-competing groups. If there is an inequality in the political rights of different racial groups there will be a tendency for their economic opportunities to be unequal, the race with less rights being restricted to the less well-paid occupations.

35. 4. *The Family* (including Marriage).

The Family is a group of persons, related by kinship, and bound by obligations of mutual support. The institution serves three economic ends: it assures the support—

    (i) Of children before they are capable of supporting themselves.

    (ii) Of women while they are bearing and rearing children.

    (iii) Of adults in sickness and old age.

Different forms of the family group are described: the polyandrous; the polygynous; the joint-family; the monogamic group of father, mother and children.

36. Marriage is the social institution regulating the permanent union of the sexes. It is usually intimately associated with the institution of the Family.

37. The Family is bound up with the economic differentiation of the sexes. The relative economic position of men and women depends on the relative importance of their economic rôles within the family. In a rationalised and individualised society these differences are reflected in differences of personal income and are transmitted, by the influence of competition, from wives to women in general.

38. Since men and women are two sexes of one species and not two separate species, differences between the economic status of the sexes cannot give rise to a division into classes, castes or orders. Where such a division already occurs, the Family tends to perpetuate them. Parents transmit a large part of their economic advantages or disadvantages to their children. This is particularly marked where there is a differential birth-rate, in the sense that the richest families have the fewest children.

39. 5. *Education.*—Education is the process of fitting individuals for the position they are to occupy in the social system. It consists of two parts:—

    (1) general preparation for membership of society and of a given community with its traditions and ethos.

    (2) special preparation for a particular status or function.

40. The economic importance of education is threefold:—

    (i) Its efficiency in developing the productive powers of a community.

    (ii) Its tendency to stereotype existing class divisions, or on the other hand, to promote economic mobility.

    (iii) The method of providing for its cost.

41. Education is tending to assume many functions previously performed by the Family. The result of this may be the 'de-institutionalising' of the latter; i.e. the reduction of the Family to a centre of purely individual relations.

42. 6. *Religion.*—The purely economic significance of Religion may be considered under two heads, the direct and the indirect influence of Religion in economic life.

43.   (i) The direct economic influence of Religion. This was greatest when magic or religion was bound up with food-getting technique. Even after that stage was passed, priestly castes continued to be paid for spiritual services; hence the importance of tithes as a source of income.

44.   (ii) The indirect economic influence of Religion is due to connections between Religion and other social institutions. They occur: (*a*) when Religion acts as a buttress to other institutions; (*b*) when Religion is organised into corporations that own and manage property; (*c*) when Religion becomes associated with an ethical code that sanctions forms of conduct that have economic significance.

45. Religion is becoming de-institutionalised. It is ceasing to be a social institution and becoming a purely private matter. Its most important economic effect is in association with certain ethical standards.

CHAPTER III

THEORY OF VALUE

1. The analysis of Value falls into two main parts:—

    (1) Use-Value, Individual Value or Subjective Value,
    (2) Exchange-Value, Social Value or Objective Value.

Exchange-Value is derived from Use-Value.

2. 1. *Use-Value.*—The use-value of a good is derived from the needs whose satisfaction is dependent on disposal of the good. Thus value is derived from need and scarcity.

3. The use-value of any one of a collection of similar goods is that of the good satisfying the least important need. This is the marginal good and its use-value is the marginal use-value (marginal utility) of the kind of good in question. The use-value of the whole collection is the marginal use-value multiplied by the number of goods. As the number of goods increases the importance of the marginal need declines and the use-value of one good falls. (Law of Diminishing Use-Value or Diminishing Marginal Utility.)

4. Justification of the assumption of economic rationality.

5. An economic subject will increase his supply of a good that is for any reason scarce (i.e. limited in relation to need) until its use-value falls to zero, when the good ceases to be an economic good. If the good is scarce its use-value will have a determinate magnitude. Supply and Demand are seen to be identical with scarcity and need.

6. Orders of goods: goods used for immediate satisfaction are goods of the first order, goods used for making them are goods of the second order, and so on with higher orders. The use-value of higher-order goods is derived from that of the lower-order goods into which they enter (Imputed Value). The law of Diminishing Value applies to goods of higher orders.

7. Definition of Joint and Composite Demand.

8. Composite Demand. The value of a good in composite demand is derived from the value of the good in its marginal use.

9. Cost. Disutility cost and Opportunity-cost.

10. Costs are the values of higher-order goods, in both composite and joint demand.

11. Alternative uses of goods are balanced and goods are so allocated to different uses as to equalise their value in these uses.

12. Defence of the so-called psychological subtleties of the theory of Use-Value.

13. 2. *Exchange-Value.*—Exchange adds to the power of an individual to satisfy his wants. Exchange implies the existence of desire for the goods exchanged; hence Exchange-Value is derived from Use-Value. Exchange implies organised society and social institutions.

14. The Subjective or Individual Exchange-Value of a good is the use-value of the goods that can be obtained in exchange for it.

15. A good produced for exchange and not for use is a Commodity. Goods disposable in exchange are Purchasing Power. Commodities and Purchasing Power are correlative terms.

16. Under conditions of a perfect market and economic rationality it is possible to adjust the consumption of different kinds of commodities so as to obtain equal satisfaction at the margin of use of each. Corresponding to this general level of satisfaction there is a use-value of purchasing power, or income, which obeys the same law as the use-value of goods, i.e. the greater the income the lower the use-value of a single unit thereof. (Cf. § 3.)

17. The Subjective Exchange-Value of a commodity varies directly with its Use-Value and inversely with the Use-Value of income.

18. Price-formation in a market. In a market there is a uniform Objective or Social Exchange-Value for all similar commodities at a given moment of time. There is a relation between this Objective Exchange-Value and the quantity of the commodity in the market.

19. The Objective or Social Exchange-Value of a commodity is that Value at which the number of goods offered is equal to the number of goods taken. It is a function of this quantity.

20. Objective Demand-Price is the price at which the whole supply is absorbed by a market. It is equal to the marginal buyer's Subjective Exchange-Value. It is a function of the quantity demanded. A list of quantities with the corresponding demand-prices is a demand schedule.

21. Objective Demand-Price diminishes as the quantity offered for sale increases.

22. Elasticity of Demand. The demand for a commodity is elastic or inelastic according as increase in the quantity offered increases or diminishes the aggregate value of the supply.

23. The Objective Supply-Price is the price which will elicit the supply of a given quantity of a commodity to a market. When production is carried on for the market there is no Subjective Supply-Price. In this case Objective Supply-Price is determined by Cost-Price, which is considered later (section 31).

24. There is a close parallel between subjective use-value and objective exchange-value. The latter plays the same rôle in Social economy as the former does in Individual economy.

25. While Subjective Exchange-Value is derived from Subjective Use-Value, we cannot argue back from Objective-Exchange-Value to the existence of an Objective or Social Use-Value. In the determination of Objective Exchange-Values there enter in not only the utilities of goods to consumers, but also consumers' money-incomes. Hence in a society exhibiting great inequalities in wealth prices are but a distorted reflection of social needs.

26. Production for the market involves the activity of the business organiser who acting under the stimulus of prices adjusts the quantity produced, combines the commodities of higher order so as to produce the ultimate commodities, and substitutes one commodity for another.

27. Imputation of Value. The value of lower-order commodities is imputed to the commodities of higher-order that go to produce them.

28. Composite Demand. A commodity in composite demand tends to be allotted to different uses so as to make equal the values imputed to it in all its different uses. Two cases occur: (i) the commodity can be allotted to different uses in varying proportions; (ii) the commodity is allotted in fixed proportions. In (i) the quantity employed in each case can be varied; in (ii) the total quantity of the commodity used must be adjusted so as to equalise values at the margin.

29. Joint Demand. Two cases occur: (i) the constitutents can be combined only in fixed proportions, (ii) the constituents can be combined in variable proportions. In case (i) valuation is only possible if the constituents have alternative uses. Two methods are available:—

    (a) If a constituent has an alternative use it has a direct value imputed to it from that use.

    (b) If the other constituents have alternative uses it has a residual value, due to the greater value that the other goods have in combination with it.

In case (ii) in addition to the above two, a third method is available, (c) by marginal net products. The marginal net product of a constituent is the net additional product obtainable by using one additional unit of that constituent, the quantity used of the others remaining constant. If none of the goods has an alternative value and the proportions in which they combine cannot be varied, their value as separate goods is indeterminate.

30. The law of diminishing Demand-Price is true of higher-order commodities as well as of first-order commodities, in complex as in simple cases of demand.

31. Costs. A cost is the value of a higher-order commodity that is both in composite and joint demand. Such a good is called a cost-good. Its value is ultimately derived by imputation from the value of its marginal use, but this value then enters into the value of all its other uses. The value of a joint product has a lower limit in the form of the sum of the values of its components. Hence arises the ordinary idea of a cost and a cost-price. This social or objective cost is analogous with the opportunity-cost of individual economy, rather than with disutility-cost.

32. Objective supply-price is determined by cost-price. The value of freely reproducible commodities tends to fall to their cost.

33. The coincidence of value and cost ensures equalisation of the marginal values of all cost goods and the optimum use of resources.

34. Restriction. If the production of a commodity is restricted, its value does not necessarily sink to its cost and there may be a permanent surplus of value above cost.

35. Three kinds of Restriction (which must be distinguished from Scarcity) are noted:—

    (i) Due to natural irreproducibility (e.g. land).

    (ii) Due to ordinary monopoly (combination of sellers).

    (iii) Due to action of social institutions.

The latter form is called Institutional Restriction.

CHAPTER IV

THEORY OF FACTOR-DISTRIBUTION

1. The ultimate cost-goods, the goods of highest order, are the factors of production. Since they can be substituted for one another within a wide range of possible proportions they may be valued by the method of marginal net products. To the supplier of a factor of production its value is his income; hence the income derived from a factor of production is determined by its marginal net product.

2. A classification of factors of production is difficult because they are numerous and not uniform. There are numerous kinds and grades of labour, land and instrumental goods. Factors must be grouped into certain main divisions.

3. The first broad distinction is between Man and Nature: the activity of the economic subject on the one hand and the not-yet-worked-on objects of the environment on the other. Man here includes man-made instrumental goods, but once these have come into existence they resemble natural objects in many respects and it is frequently difficult to distinguish between natural and artificial instruments of production. Hence a different line of division between Work and Instruments. We thus get a threefold division into Labour, Capital and Land. These must be considered not so much as single factors of production but as convenient names for groups of factors.

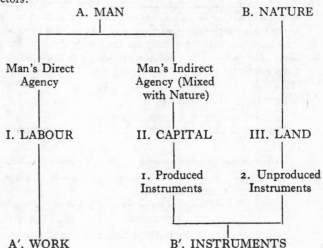

The use of produced instruments of production involves two elements: the Waiting, on which depends their coming into existence, and the Uncertainty-bearing, which necessarily attends their productive use.

The main groups of factors of production, with the names that are given to their returns, are:—

I. Labour			Wages.
II. Capital	{	1. Waiting	Interest.
		2. Uncertainty-bearing	Profit.
III. Land			Rent.

4. I. *Labour.*—Labour may be defined as personal activity of economic significance. Its return is Wages, including not only wages in the usual sense but salaries, fees, commissions and the earnings of the self-employed worker.

5. Different kinds of Labour may be classified in two ways:—

  A. Horizontally, by industry and trade.
  B. Vertically, by grade of skill or responsibility:

    (i) unskilled manual labour.
    (ii) skilled manual labour and mental labour not involving responsibility.
    (iii) responsible and specialised mental labour.
    (iv) creative labour.

6. The Demand for Labour. The demand for any kind of labour is derived from its marginal net product, which fixes an amount more than which that labour will not, in the long run, be able to obtain. This is true, not only for the wage-labourer, but for the slave, for the serf and for the self-employed worker. It is not fundamentally altered by the existence of collective bargaining.

7. The Supply of Labour:—

  A. The Supply of Labour as a whole.
  The supply of labour as a whole can be increased in three ways:—

    (i) increase in the numbers of the occupied population—

      (*a*) growth in the numbers of the sex and age groups normally occupied.
      (*b*) extension of employment to sex and age groups not previously occupied.

    (ii) extension of the working time of those already occupied.

(iii) increase in the intensity or efficiency of labour during hours of work.

Only in case (iii) does there seem to be any such connection between the price of labour (wages) and the supply forthcoming as can be described as a supply schedule. In cases (i) and (ii) there seems to be no tendency for supply to respond in any definite way to changes in the wage offered. The 'brazen law of wages' is untenable as a general theory of wages. Labour as a whole has no supply price and the return to Labour is of the nature of rent.

8. B. *The Supply of particular kinds of Labour.* The supply of labour to particular trades and grades responds to changes in the wages offered. These do not affect the total supply of labour, but determine its allocation to particular uses. There is thus a definite supply price for particular kinds of labour. This applies more particularly to the middle grades and less to unskilled labour and to creative labour, both of which, for different reasons, have no supply price.

9. Certain kinds of human activity give rise to special problems in the theory of distribution. They are those of the persons who work the organisations that embody certain social institutions, especially those of Labour Organisation, the Organisation of Enterprise, and Government. These persons are often in a position to sell their services under monopoly conditions.

10. (*a*) *Labour Organisation.*—Labour organisation is a function with a certain economic value, but like business organisation it may come to exercise monopoly power. When labour organisations exercise such power the monopoly revenue usually appears in the form of a monopoly element in their members' wages rather than in the incomes of the organisers themselves.

11. (*b*) *Organisation of Enterprise.*—The demand for the services of the business organiser depends on his marginal net product. The supply depends on the same influences as that of other kinds of special ability. Education, in the widest sense, including all opportunities for getting experience of men and affairs, economic freedom, and the different forms of business organisation, affect the supply.

12. *Business Monopoly.*—The business organiser is in a favourable position for the exercise of monopoly power. He can, by restricting output, raise price above cost. This surplus, multiplied by the number of units sold, is his net monopoly-revenue.

13. Two stages are theoretically possible in the development of monopoly power in industry.

(1) It is confined to particular industries. In this case it drives factors of production out of the monopolised into the non-monopolised industries and thus lowers their marginal net product: the total social product is reduced but the monopolists acquire a larger absolute share.

(2) It is general, not in the sense that there is particular monopoly in every industry (which would produce an unstable condition) but in the sense of a monopolistic organisation of all production so as to maximise the income of the class that controls industry. The result would be a lower social product than the maximum attainable, a lowered marginal net product of all non-monopolised factors of production, but factors of production would be allocated to the different branches of industry in the most suitable manner for the given level of production.

General monopoly is illustrated by a discussion of the distribution of product between two non-competing groups.

14. (c) *Government.*—The state has a right to be considered a factor of production. It is a productive force, with a cost, expressed in taxes, and other payments, and with a marginal net product. It is worth while for a community to extend its expenditure on governmental functions up to the point at which their net addition to social income is just covered by their cost in taxes, etc. Under modern conditions the provision of these functions is a public monopoly, but in other times it was privately provided and its return was a constituent in individual income. Thus part of the income of a feudal lord was the proceeds of state functions, privately performed.

15. II. *Capital.*—The return to capital is not adequately explained by the physical productivity of instrumental goods, for it would be expected that, in accordance with the law of derived value, the whole value of the product would be imputed to the goods that entered into it, leaving no surplus of value at all. The explanation of the surplus, which is the return to capital, is to be found in the time-relations of production. These have two aspects, physical and psychological.

A. Physical. Capitalist production yields a high product at the cost of a lapse of time between the first steps in production and the consumption of the product. Their lapse of time involves two things:—

(i) Someone must wait for the product;
(ii) There is uncertainty whether the product will be wanted when it is ready.

B. Psychological.

>   (i) People prefer present goods to future goods, and hence
>   are unwilling to wait;
>
>   (ii) Uncertainty as to the value of the product makes people
>   unwilling to expose their resources to the risk involved in
>   the productive use thereof.

Thus Capital resolves itself into the two functions of Waiting
and Uncertainty-Bearing.

16. (i) *Waiting.*—The preference for present goods over future ones
can be attributed to three main causes: (*a*) the less vivid realisation
of future needs; (*b*) the relation between needs and provision for
needs at different periods in the individual's life; (*c*) the uncertainty
of income at different periods of life. Any one of these usually
causes future goods to be undervalued. While future goods can
only be enjoyed in the future, present goods can usually be stored
for future use; hence the discount on future goods due to any
of these causes will rarely sink below zero. These three causes
are cumulative: therefore most individuals have a preference for
present goods over future goods of the same physical quantity
and description. This preference is called a time-preference.
Generally speaking, the poorer an individual the higher is the
rate at which he discounts future goods.

17. Collective bodies as well as individuals have a definite time-
preference. (For interest in a socialist state, see Appendix to
Chapter IV.) The time-preference of a group depends on the
same factors as that of an individual, but tends to be lower
than that of the members of the group in their individual capacity,
(*a*) because when the group acquires a sense of collective personality the uncertainty of life exercises less strong an influence
and (*b*) because an individual can be persuaded more easily to
forgo something that is due to him but that he has never handled
than to forgo something that has passed into his effective
possession.

18. Out of different individuals' subjective time-preferences there
emerges, by the higgling of the market, an objective time-preference, embodied in a market rate of interest. The process is
exactly parallel to the development of Objective Exchange-Value
out of Subjective Use-Value.

19. Since individuals' subjective time-preferences are various and
differ from the market rate of interest, some people are willing
to lend and some to borrow. In general it is the rich who are

lenders and the poor who are borrowers. This is not contradicted by the fact that entrepreneurs are the chief borrowers, because they borrow not on their own account but on that of consumers and labourers, who are the ultimate borrowers. (Wages are advances to labourers and the discounted marginal product of labour.)

20. Waiting (or saving) makes possible an accumulation of resources which can be used for financing roundabout and time-consuming, but ultimately more productive, methods of production. Thus we can identify Waiting with produced means of production and the return to Waiting with the marginal net product of such means of production.

21. The demand for Waiting is derived from its marginal net product, that is to say from the marginal net product of instruments of production. Owing to the law of diminishing returns, and to the diminishing marginal utility of first-order goods, the marginal net product of instruments of production falls as the quantity available increases. Hence the demand-price for capital falls as a community grows richer.

22. The supply of Waiting depends on the time-preference of the marginal saver. This in turn depends on:—
    (a) total wealth of the community;
    (b) its distribution;
    (c) the prevalent forms of Property;
    (d) the habits and customs of the people
    (a) The greater the total wealth of the community the greater the supply of Waiting.
    (b) Inequality of wealth has two opposite effects: (a) rich people set a high standard of expenditure, which diminishes the investable surplus; (β) owing to the lower time-preference of rich people a given rate of interest will elicit more saving from a community in which wealth is unequally distributed than from one in which the same amount of wealth per head is more equally distributed. It is possible that, in modern communities with their competitive standards of ostentation, effect (a) is predominant over (β) and that on the whole inequality lowers the supply of saving.
    (c) Associative property, especially public property, is more favourable to saving than individual property.

23. (ii) *Uncertainty-Bearing.*—Owing to the diminishing marginal utility of resources the certainty of one pound has greater sub-

jective value than the equal probability of two pounds or nothing. Hence the exposure of resources to risk involves a loss of utility and investments involving uncertainty will tend to be valued at less than their actuarial value.

24. Risks are of two kinds: insurable and non-insurable. The former are destroyed by aggregation; the latter are not. It is the latter kind of risk that is involved in the economic function of uncertainty-bearing. Such risks are inevitable if production is to be carried on in anticipation of demand, especially by capitalist methods.

25. The Demand for Uncertainty-Bearing. The demand for this function depends on:—

- (*a*) the number and variety of commodities offered to consumers.
- (*b*) the prevalence of changes of fashion or taste.
- (*c*) the prevalence of technical inventions and new methods of organisation.
- (*d*) the extent of specialisation in industry.
- (*e*) the extent of the market.
- (*f*) the methods of industrial organisation, whether competitive or co-ordinated.

26. The Supply of Uncertainty-Bearing. The supply of this function depends on the same causes as that of waiting, but individual differences of temperament are more important here. The supply of uncertainty-bearing is therefore increased by any device, such as the division of shares into ordinary and preference, that enables investors of different temperaments to choose the degree of risk that they prefer.

27. The worker, as well as the entrepreneur, bears uncertainty. Given mobility of labour, wages tend to include return on this function. If labour is not mobile the worker will be insufficiently compensated for fluctuation in earnings. Owing to the lowness of his income the worker is not in a position to bear uncertainty well. Hence anything that diminishes fluctuation in earnings benefits him. (1) Unemployment Insurance shifts uncertainty on to shoulders better capable of bearing it. Insurance by industry is compared with national insurance. (2) Co-partnership and profit-sharing schemes are open to the objection that by associating the worker with the fortunes of a particular firm they increase the variability of income.

28. *Business Profits.*—Business profits are hard to classify. After deductions from the business organiser's earnings of Interest, Rent and Wages of management or superintendence, there remain four elements:—

> (1) Pure profit (the returns to Uncertainty-Bearing).
> (2) Conjuncture-gains.
> (3) Differential-gains.
> (4) Monopoly-gains.

29. Capital considered (1) as a historical category, (2) as a technical factor.

30. III. *Land.*—The return to Land is determined entirely by the demand for it. It can be considered from two points of view, known respectively as the Differential and the Scarcity Theories of Rent.

> (i) The Differential Theory of Rent derives Rent from the different returns of equal amounts of human activity applied to different pieces of land.
> (ii) The Scarcity Theory of Rent treats Rent as the return to a factor of production that is limited in quantity. This return is a surplus of price over cost.

These two theories are really aspects of one theory, according to which the return to land is the marginal net product of a naturally restricted factor of production. Rent is part of some person's income: the ultimate appropriation of it is a matter for the next chapter.

31. Review of the theory of Marginal Net Products. 'Marginal uses indicate, they do not govern value.' The forces that determine the position of the margin can be divided into two sets: (1) those affecting the conditions of demand: (2) those affecting the conditions of supply. This division is formal rather than realistic.

32. General Theory of Demand for Factors of Production.
The demand-price of a factor of production is determined by its marginal net product. This latter is defined as the extra value added to the product when one more unit of the factor is utilised. It depends on the number of units already in use. Therefore, the marginal net product and hence the demand-price of a factor is a function of the quantity available.

33. This theory is subject to two qualifications.

(1) Under private enterprise the limit to which it is profitable to push the use of a factor of production or of factors in general does not always coincide with the margin determined on the basis of market prices. This is due to three causes:—

(a) deficient bargaining power of supplies of some factors,

(b) monopoly,

(c) open or concealed taxes and subsidies.

We can thus distinguish marginal social net product from marginal trade net product and from marginal individual net product according as the disturbing causes affect whole industries or single businesses.

(2) Inequality of individual incomes makes market price a distorted index of social need.

34. General Theory of Supply of Factors of Production.

Some factors have and some have not a definite supply-price in the sense that the quantity available is a function of the price. Some Capital and many kinds of labour have a supply-price: Land, and some Capital and some kinds of labour, including the simplest as well as the most complex, have none. Although some kinds of labour have a supply-price, Labour as a whole has none.

35. Marginal Net Product may be affected from the supply side. Any cause that restricts the supply of a factor raises its return relative to that of other, unrestricted or less restricted, factors. This it does in two ways: (i) the scarcity of the factor raises the margin of its profitable application and so increases its marginal net product absolutely; (ii) the other factors, being forced into other uses, have their marginal net products lowered.

36. The fundamental principle in factor distribution is that of rent. Where economic life is carried on along prescribed lines this principle holds good immediately for each factor. Where economic rationality exists an economic subject can, within certain limits, adjust his supply of different factors so as to maximise his total income. These limits are those of his total opportunity of income-getting. The rent principle now applies, not to any particular factor, but to the total number of units of opportunity at the subject's disposal. An individual's opportunities are partly a function of his abilities and partly a function of the social institutions that environ him. Under perfect mobility and freedom of choice the number of such units depends on the subjects' abilities; social institutions that restrict mobility and freedom introduce arbitrary variations into the number of opportunity units.

Appendix: Interest in a Socialist Community.

CHAPTER V

THE THEORY OF PERSONAL DISTRIBUTION

1. The income of an individual is equal to the product of the number of factors of production at his disposal into the average yield of the factors. The latter depends on the marginal net product of such factors and has been discussed in Chapter IV. The former is usually neglected in works in distribution but consideration of it is necessary to the elucidation of the forces governing total personal income.

2. Under conditions of equal opportunity the returns on equal natural abilities would tend to equality. But in societies as they are actually constituted all persons do not enjoy equal opportunities. Society can be divided into groups characterised by equality of opportunity within the groups and inequality of opportunity between groups. These are called 'noncompeting groups'. They may be based on distinctions of race or sex or on differences of caste, order or class. Those based on differences of class are defined roughly by income limits and more precisely by opportunities of obtaining education and control over capital.

3. Under existing conditions in this country we may distinguish five non-competing groups :—
    (1) Upper Class.
    (2) Upper Middle Class.
    (3) Lower Middle Class.
    (4) Skilled Working Class.
    (5) Unskilled Working Class.
These groups are defined and discussed.

4. The composition of a group and the opportunities enjoyed by a typical member of it depend on the institutions of Property (including Contract and Inheritance), Education and Economic Freedom. The distribution of wealth between members of the same group follows the principle of marginal productivity: dis-

tribution between groups follows that of international exchange. Within a group income tends to be proportional to ability and industry, while as between different groups individual income depends on institutional causes which determine the number of opportunity-units that fall to the lot of the typical member of a group.

5. The theory here set forth can be attacked in two ways:—
    (1) By denying the existence of non-competing groups.
    (2) By denying the institutional basis of such groups, while admitting their existence.

6. (1) To deny the existence of non-competing groups is to assert the existence of complete mobility and free choice of occupation for persons of all social classes. Some mobility certainly exists: our society is not rigidly stratified into orders or castes. Nevertheless there are great differences in the opportunities of different classes. (For statistical references, see Appendix to Chapter V.)

7. (2) Those who, while they admit the existence of non-competing groups, deny their institutional basis, usually attribute them to inherent differences in quality between human beings. This is unlikely (i) because it is uncertain whether specific qualities of social ability can be inherited; (ii) because the present system of competitive individualism arose out of a system of Orders and civil inequality; (iii) because windfalls and anti-windfalls may throw individuals up or down the scale; (iv) because families ramify so extensively.

8. Non-competing groups are maintained by barriers that hinder mobility. These are of three kinds : (1) ignorance of opportunities, (2) cost of movement, (3) social institutions. When (1) and (2) are important it is usually because they are cases of (3). A fourth barrier—physical force—is suggested, but this, if it is effective, always implies the existence of a social institution. Social institutions are, therefore, the chief generators of non-competing groups.

9. The theory here put forward is that social institutions generate non-competing groups, that they secure for the more favoured of these groups, Institutional Restriction of certain factors of production, and that the earnings of members of such groups contain an element akin to net monopoly of revenue. This element might be called Net Institutional Restriction Revenue, but it will be called simply Institutional Revenue.

10. We will consider the chief factors of production and their respective returns.

11. I. *Labour—Wages.*
Institutional Revenue enters into the earnings of the skilled workman and the professional man. Its cause is limitation of supply, effected in two ways:—

(1) accumulated resources required to enter occupation, owing to

(*a*) long and expensive training;
(*b*) possession of capital being inseparable from practice of calling;
(*c*) long non-earning period at beginning of career.

(2) Activity of trade associations—

(*a*) demarcation rules;
(*b*) regulation of number of apprentices;
(*c*) prohibition of labour-saving methods;
(*d*) enforcement of high minimum wage.

(3) institutions which produce a complete fixity of supply—

(*a*) gilds;
(*b*) caste;
(*c*) legal or traditional segregation of the sexes or of members of different races with respect to industrial occupation.

12. Labour may permanently be paid less than its marginal net product—

A. in a particular trade:—
in two cases:—

(1) Monopoly, accompanied by absence of alternative employment for workmen in non-monopolised trades.
(2) Institutional Restriction of entrepreneur function in that trade.

B. in all trades:—
when there is Restriction of the entrepreneur function generally.

13. Labour may be paid more than its marginal net product—

A. in particular trades:—

when there is an association of workpeople capable of restricting entry into the trade. They then enjoy an

Institutional Restriction of their labour and their earnings contain an element of Institutional Revenue.

B. in all trades:—

when the working class as a class, through the exercise of political power,

 (1) forces employers to keep their establishments going at a loss or employ more men than they can profitably find work for;

 (2) keeps wages above their normal level, the workmen who are permanently unemployed as a consequence being maintained out of public money.

14. *Earnings of Labour specially involved in the working of Institutions* (Cf. Chapter IV, section 9).

15. (*a*) *Business Organisation and its Earnings*.

The returns to business organisation often contain an element of Institution Revenue for two reasons:—

 (1) the necessity to the business aspirant of costly training or of some kind of 'influence';

 (2) the necessity of having some capital of his own.

16. *Monopoly Profits.*—Net monopoly revenue is not the earnings of any factor of production and is purely Institutional Revenue. It is closely associated with the earnings of Enterprise.

17. (*b*) *Government and its Earnings*.

Nowadays public authorities (states and municipalities) maintain a monopoly of the function of Government and supply it at cost. It does not, therefore, give rise to any Institutional Revenue. Under the feudal system it was supplied by individuals, belonging to a privileged Order, who made what profit they could out of it. Their income contained a large element of Institutional Revenue.

18. The theory of 'income of sovereignty' (Herrschaftseinkommen) is examined and such income shown to be a form of Institutional Revenue.

19. Income from Civil Rights is considered. It is of two kinds:—

 (1) involving a redistribution of income within the same non-competing group;

 (2) involving a transference from one non-competing group to another.

In case (1) it contains Institutional Revenue in so far as the income of the group involves Institutional Revenue. In case (2) it is a transference due to the exercise of political power ('income of sovereignty') and contains Institutional Revenue to the extent that the power in question effects an Institutional Restriction.

20. II. *Capital.*

(*a*) Waiting —Interest. Under a system of private property and free enterprise, a large part of the social product that is needed for further production is paid over to individuals, who are then tempted, by the offer of interest, to use it productively (i.e. to save it). This has two effects:—

> (1) provision of the factor of Waiting is confined to a small number of comparatively wealthy persons and thus the return per person tends to be high;
> (2) the time-preference of the marginal saver is probably higher than that of the community as a whole would be.

Thus there is an Institutional Restriction of Waiting and even the marginal saver receives Institutional Revenue.

21. (*b*) Uncertainty-Bearing—Profit. The earnings of Uncertainty-Bearing contain an element of Institutional Revenue for three reasons:—

> (1) a large part of uncertainty is created by the competitive individualistic organisation of economic activity;
> (2) the bearing of it is limited to those with considerable resources to expose, i.e. to the wealthy.
> (3) the same probability of loss, though compensated for at the same rate, involves a smaller loss of utility to the richer man than to the poorer.

22. III. *Land—Rent.*

Land and natural resources are comparatively fixed in quantity and are thus an example of natural restriction: on the basis of this an Institutional Restriction is created by permitting them to become private property. The private ownership of land and the private appropriation of the return thereof are not based on any economic necessity, since rent is not a supply-price; they are purely institutional creations. Hence individual income drawn from such ownership is purely Institutional Revenue.

23. *Capitalisation of Income.*

The rate of Interest is a ratio between a capital sum and an annual income. Under institutions that permit regular investment for profit and free interchange of different kinds of income-yielding property, all regular annual sources of income can be capitalised. Thus incomes from ownership of land and capital and business opportunities involving monopoly or exceptional advantages become mutually convertible and merged into the general category of Income from Property. It is then shown that all Institutional Revenue—that flowing from institutionally restricted kinds of Labour as well as Rent, Interest, Profit and Monopoly Revenue—can be capitalised.

24. *Work-Incomes and Property-Incomes.*

The distinction between incomes derived from Work and those derived from Property is important. The chief difference between them is that the former are inherently personal and are non-transferable, while the latter are merely attributed to particular persons by virtue of social conventions and are in general transferable to others. Two consequences flow from this distinction, both of which tend to limit the number of receivers of Institutional Revenue.

25. (1) Inheritance tends to produce an exclusive and limited class of hereditarily wealthy persons who have exceptional opportunities of adding to their wealth.

26. (2) Owing to the limits of human effort on the one hand and the diminishing marginal utility of income on the other, Work-incomes can only be increased with progressive difficulty, while Property-incomes can be increased with regressive difficulty. Thus Property-incomes tend to increase more rapidly than Work-incomes.

27. There is inherent therefore, in an individualistic society, a constant and cumulative force which tends to make the rich richer, and the poor, at least relatively, poorer. This tendency can be counteracted by progressive direct taxation, but such taxation has its limits, which are reached when it impairs the supply of Waiting and Uncertainty-Bearing.

28. Objects of Property can be divided into:—

(1) Rights in consumption goods.
(2) Claims on society for income (corresponding approximately to the category of production goods).

It is suggested that a limitation of the scope of property and inheritance with respect to the latter would do much to diminish inequality of income.

29. *Rent of Ability.*

Rent of Ability is defined as the return to special personal qualities that cannot be produced by training and that happen to have high economic value. It is the resultant of a natural, not an institutional restriction, and does not include any Institutional Revenue.

30. *Conjuncture-Gains.*

Conjuncture-gains are defined as income arising from unforeseen changes in the economic situation. Much of them cancel out in the long run but in a progressive society some remain. They are to be considered as Institutional Revenue or not according to the circumstances that give rise to them and to the form of their appropriation. If they do not contain Institutional Revenue they are called Pure Conjuncture-Gains and can be classed along with Rent of Ability as Personal Rent.

31. *Basic Earnings.*—Income that is not Institutional Revenue, or Personal Rent may be called Basic Earnings.

32. We thus get a twofold classification of Income-categories.

A. STATIC.	B. DYNAMIC.
I. Wages.	1. Basic Earnings.
IIa. Interest.	2. Personal Rent.
IIb. Profit.	3. Institutional Revenue.
III. Rent.	

Appendix:—Statistical Evidence for the Existence of Non-competing Groups.

CHAPTER VI

SOME CRITICISMS OF THE THEORY OF INSTITUTIONAL REVENUE

1. That it implies that some income is institutional and some not, whereas all income is due to social institutions. But Institutional Revenue means that part of income which is due to an Institutional Restriction of some factor of production. All income is institutional but not all is Institutional Revenue in this sense.

2. That all income involves Institutional Revenue since all social institutions involve Restriction. This objection is based on a verbal confusion between Restriction in the sense of a restraint in activity and Restriction in the technical sense here given to it of a limitation in the supply of a factor of production.

3. That the concept of Institutional Revenue implies a comparison of existing conditions with a hypothetical state of affairs in which there is no Institutional Restriction. This is admitted. The hypothetical standard of comparison is either the ideal individualistic or the ideal communistic society. Both involve perfect equality of opportunity and the absence of economic classes. Institutional Restriction has been shown to have the same connotation as Inequality of Opportunity. The ideal society in which there is no Institutional Restriction is compared with the ideal communistic society of Wieser's *Natural Value*.

CHAPTER VII

SOME APPLICATIONS OF THE THEORY OF INSTITUTIONAL REVENUE

1. *Historical.*—The incidence of Institutional Revenue is not arbitrary. Every social system is characterised by certain institutions and these involve certain kinds of Institutional Restriction. Changes in social institutions are correlated with changes in the incidence of Institutional Revenue. Thus this concept may be used in historical or sociological analysis.

   Although the theory of Institutional Revenue does not necessarily involve the Marxian theory of history, it can be used in connection with it, taking the place of the concept of Surplus-Value.

2. *Critical.*—The argument of this book tends to demolish the idea that there is anything particularly 'natural' about a social system based on laisser-faire individualism or that in the distribution of wealth under such a system each individual obtains just what he produces. No ethical judgment is implied in the concept of Institutional Revenue.

3. *Practical.*—The bearing of Institutional Revenue is examined upon projects of social change tending to reduce the inequalities of wealth.

BIBLIOGRAPHY

This bibliography contains (i) books which have influenced the development of the author's views, (ii) a few works which the author has not read but are referred to in the books included above, (iii) all the works referred to in the text.

Where a reference is give thus: 1910 (1920), the date in brackets refers to a subsequent revised and/or enlarged edition.

Abbreviations: E.J. *Economic Journal.*
J.P.E. *Journal of Political Economy.*
J.R.S.S. *Journal of the Royal Statistical Society.*
Q.J.E. *Quarterly Journal of Economics.*

I. SOCIOLOGY AND SOCIAL INSTITUTIONS

A. GENERAL SOCIOLOGY

Plato: *The Republic.*
C. de S. Montesquieu: *L'Esprit des Lois,* 1748.
H. T. Buckle: *The History of Civilization in England,* 1857–61.
H. Maine: *Ancient Law,* 1861 (1884).
W. Bagehot: *Physics and Politics,* 1872.
A. Wagner: *Grundlegung der Politischen Ökonomie,* 1879.
E. T. Rogers: *The Economic Interpretation of History,* 1858.
E. R. A. Seligman: *The Economic Interpretation of History,* 1902 (1924).
G. Wallas: *The Great Society,* 1914.
R. M. Maciver: *Community,* 1917.
G. D. H. Cole: *Social Theory,* 1920.
F. Oppenheimer: *System der Soziologie,* 1922.
M. Weber: *Wirtschaft und Gesellschaft,* 1922 (Band III of *Grundriss der Soziolökonomik,* by various authors).
N. Bukharin: *Historical Materialism,* Translated from the Russian, 1925.

B. WORKS ON PARTICULAR INSTITUTIONS

1. LABOUR ORGANISATION

W. S. Jevons: *The State in Relation to Labour,* 1882 (1914).
B. and S. Webb: *Industrial Democracy,* 1902 (1920).
G. D. H. Cole: *Organised Labour,* 1924.

2. Industrial Organisation

K. Bücher: *Die Entstehung der Volkswirtschaft*, 1893 (Trans. *Industrial Evolution*, 1901).
R. W. Liefmann: *Unternehmer-Verbände*, 1897.
    Beteiligungs und Finanzierungs-gesellschaften, 1909 (1931).
    Kartelle und Trusts, 1910. (Reprinted as *Kartelle, Konzerne und Trusts*, 1927.)
J. W. Jenks: *The Trust Problem*, 1900 (1912).
G. Unwin: *Industrial Organization in the Sixteenth and Seventeenth Centuries*, 1904.
D. H. Macgregor: *Industrial Combination*, 1906.
H. Levy: *Monopole, Kartelle und Trusts*, 1909. (Trans. *Monopoly and Competition*, 1911.)
R. Hilferding: *Finanzkapital*, 1912 (1927).
A. Marshall: *Industry and Trade*, 1919.
F. Lavington: *The English Capital Market*, 1921.
H. A. Marquand: *Dynamics of Industrial Combination*, 1931.

3. The State

Plato: *The Republic*.
Aristotle: *Politics*.
J. Locke: *A Treatise on Civil Government*, 1689.
J. J. Rousseau: *Le Contrat Social*, 1762.
J. S. Mill: *Liberty*, 1859.
    Representative Government, 1861.
H. Sidgwick: *Elements of Politics*, 1891 (1908).
J. R. Seeley: *Introduction to Political Science*, 1896.
F. Oppenheimer: *Der Staat*, 1908. (Trans. *The State*, 1913.)
L. Duguit: *Les Transformations du Droit Public*, 1913. (Trans. *Law in the Modern State*, 1921.)
E. v. Böhm-Bawerk: *Macht oder ökonomisches Gesetz?* 1914 (included in his *Gesammelte Schriften*, 1924).
H. J. Laski: *A Grammar of Politics*, 1925 (1930).
R. M. Maciver: *The Modern State*, 1926.
J. van den Tempel: *Macht en Economische Wet*, 1927.
R. G. Hawtrey: *Economic Aspects of Sovereignty*, 1930.
C. E. G. Catlin: *The Principles of Politics*, 1930.

4. Property (including Contract and Inheritance)

W. Blackstone: *Commentary on the Laws of England*, 1765–69.
J. A. Hobson: *Rights of Property* (The Free Review, I, p. 130), 1899.
T. Veblen: *Vested Interests*, 1919.
    Absentee Ownership, 1923.

R. T. Ely: *Property and Contract*, 1914 (1922).
J. R. Commons: *The Legal Foundations of Capitalism*, 1924.
J. Wedgwood: *The Economics of Inheritance*, 1929.

5. STATUS

J. S. Mill: *Liberty*, 1859.
T. Veblen: *The Theory of the Leisure Class*, 1899.
S. J. Chapman and F. J. Marquis: *The Recruiting of the Employing Classes from the Ranks of the Wage-Earners in the Cotton Industry* (J.R.S.S., LXXV, p. 293), 1912.
H. Belloc: *The Servile State*, 1913 (1927).
H. Dalton: (See GENERAL ECONOMIC THEORY).
M. Ginsberg: *Interchange between Social Classes* (E.J., XXXIX, p. 554), 1929.
R. H. Tawney: *Equality*, 1931.

6. THE FAMILY, MARRIAGE, RELATIONS OF THE SEXES

J. S. Mill: *The subjection of Women*, 1869.
A. Bebel: *Die Frau*, 1883 (1910). (Trans, *Woman*, 1885 (1915).)
E. Westermarck: *History of Human Marriage*, 1891 (1921).
O. Schreiner: *Woman and Labour*, 1911.
B. Webb ⎫
F. Y. Edgworth ⎬ See THEORY OF WAGES.
M. and M. Vaerting: *Neubegründung der Psychologie von Mann und Weib*, 1921. (Trans. *The Dominant Sex*, 1923.)
A. M. Carr-Saunders: *The Population Problem*, 1922.

7. EDUCATION

E. Ll. Lewis: *The Children of the Unskilled*, 1924.
K. Lindsay: *Social Progress and Educational Waste*, 1926.

8. RELIGION

E. Troeltsch: *Die Soziallehren der christlichen Kirchen und Gruppen*, 1911. (Trans. *The Social Teaching of the Christian Churches*, 1931.)
W. Cunningham: *Christianity and Social Science*, 1914.
Max Weber: *Gesammelte Aufsätze zur Religionssoziologie*, 1920–22.
R. H. Tawney: *Religion and the Rise of Capitalism*, 1926.

9. DEVELOPMENT OF CAPITALISM

J. A. Hobson: *Imperialism*, 1902.
The Evolution of Modern Capitalism, 1906 (1917).

W. Sombart: *Der moderne Kapitalismus*, 1902 (1916).
    Der Bourgeois, 1913. (Trans. *The Quintessence of Capitalism*, 1915.)
S. Webb: *Towards Social Democracy*, 1909 (1919).
S. Webb and B. Webb: *The Decay of Capitalist Civilisation*, 1923.
H. N. Brailsford: *The War of Steel and Gold*, 1914 (1915).
N. Lenin: *Imperialism* (First Russian ed. 1917).
R. H. Tawney: *The Acquisitive Society*, 1921.
M. Dobb: *Capitalist Enterprise and Social Progress*, 1925.

II. ECONOMICS

A. GENERAL WORKS ON ECONOMIC THEORY, VALUE AND DISTRIBUTION

1. CLASSICAL AND POST-CLASSICAL SCHOOL

A. Smith: *The Wealth of Nations*, 1776.
D. Ricardo: *The Principles of Political Economy and Taxation*, 1817.
N. W. Senior: *Political Economy*, 1836.
F. List: *Das nationale System der politischen Ökonomie*, 1841. (Trans. *The National System of Political Economy*, 1885, 1904.)
J. H. von Thünen: *Der isolirte Staat*, 1842.
J. S. Mill: *Principles of Political Economy*, 1848.
J. S. Cairnes: *Some Leading Principles of Political Economy*, 1874.

2. GERMAN HISTORICAL SCHOOL

(a) OLD HISTORICAL SCHOOL

W. G. F. Roscher: *Grundriss zu Vorlesungen über die Staatswissenschaft nach geschichtlicher Methode*, 1843.
    System der Volkswirtschaft, 1854 (1894).
B. Hildebrand: *Die Nationalökonomie der Gegenwart und Zukunft*, 1845.
K. Knies: *Die politische Ökonomie vom Standpunkt der geschichtlichen Methode*, 1853 (1883).

(b) NEW HISTORICAL SCHOOL

A. Wagner: *Grundlegung der politischen Ökonomie*, 1879 (1892).
    Teil I. *Grundlagen der Volkswirtschaft*.
    Teil II. *Volkswirtschaft und Recht*.
G. Schmoller: *Grundriss der allgemeinen Volkswirtschaftslehre*, 1901.

3. Socialist Writers

(a) Marxists and Neo-Marxists

K. Marx: *Zur Kritik der politischen Ökonomie*, 1859. (Trans. *Critique of Political Economy*, 1904.)
> *Das Kapital.*
> > Band I. *Produktionsprocess des Kapitals*, 1867.
> > Band II. *Cirkulationsprocess des Kapitals*, 1885.
> > Band III. *Gesammtprocess der kapitalistischen Produktion*, 1894.
> > (Trans. *Capital*, 3 vols., 1886–1907–1909. New translation of Vol. I, 1928.)
> *Theorien über Mehrwert*, 1905.

E. Bernstein: *Die Voraussetzungen des Marxismus*, 1899. (Trans. *Evolutionary Socialism*, 1909.)

T. Veblen: *The Theory of Business Enterprise*, 1904.

F. Oppenheimer: *Theorie der reinen und politischen Ökonomie*, 1910. (Band III of his *System der Soziologie*.)
> *Grundriss der theoretischen Ökonomik*, 1926.

A. Loria: *La Sintesi Economica*, 1909. (Trans. *The Economic Synthesis*, 1914.)

N. Bukharin: *The Economic Theory of the Leisure Class*, 1927. (First Russian ed., 1919.)

(b) Non-Marxists

H. George: *Progress and Poverty*, 1879.

J. A. Hobson: *The Economics of Distribution*, 1900.
> *The Industrial System*, 1909 (1910).

H. Dalton: *Some Aspects of the Inequality of Incomes in Modern Communities*, 1920 (1925).

A. D. Lindsay: *Karl Marx's Capital*, 1925.

4. Mathematical Economists

W. Whewell: *Mathematical Exposition of Some Doctrines of Political Economy* (Camb. Phil. Trans.), 1829, 1831, 1850.

A. Cournot: *Recherches sur les Principes Mathématiques de la Théorie des Richesses*, 1838. (Trans. 1895, 1927.)

H. H. Gossen: *Entwickelung der Gesetze des menschlichen Verkehrs, und der daraus fliessenden Regeln für menschliches Handeln*, 1854. (German ed. F. Hayek, 1927.)

F. Jenkin: *Graphical Representation of the Laws of Supply and Demand*. (*Edinburgh Phil. Trans*) 1870 (Reprint 1931).

W. S. Jevons: *Theory of Political Economy*, 1871.

L. Walras: *Principes d'une Théorie Mathématique de l'Echange*, 1873.
Eléments d'Economie Politique Pure, ou Théorie de la Richesse Sociale, 1874.
F. Y. Edgworth: *Mathematical Psychics*, 1881. (Reprint 1932.)
A. Marshall: *Principles of Economics* (Mathematical Appendix), 1890.
The Pure Theory of Domestic Values, 1897 (1930).
I. Fisher: *Mathematical Investigations into the Theory of Value and Prices*, 1892. (Reprint 1925.)
Researches into the Mathematical Principles of the Theory of Wealth, 1927.
A. L. Bowley: *Mathematical Groundwork of Economics*, 1924.
G. Cassel: *Theory of Social Economy* (chap. iv), 1923 (1932).

5. THE AUSTRIAN SCHOOL

(a) AUSTRIAN WRITERS

C. Menger: *Grundsätze der Volkswirtschaftslehre*, 1871 (1923).
F. von Wieser: *Über den Ursprung und die Hauptgesetze des wirtschaftlichen Wertes*, 1884.
Der natürliche Wert, 1889. (Trans. *Natural Value*, 1893.)
The Austrian School and the Theory of Value (E.J., I, p. 108), 1891.
Theorie der gesellschaftlichen Wirtschaft, 1914. (Trans. *Social Economics*, 1927.)
E. v. Böhm-Bawerk: *Geschichte und Kritik der Kapitalzins-theorien*, 1884. (Trans. *Capital and Interest*, 1890.)
Positive Theorie des Kapitals, 1889. (Trans. *The Positive Theory of Capital*, 1891.)
Grundzüge der Theorie des wirtschaftlichen Güterwerts (Conrads Jahrbücher), 1886. (Reprint 1932.)
Zum Abschluss des Marxschen Systems, 1896. (Trans. *Karl Marx and the Close of his System*, 1898.)
Recent Literature on Interest, 1903.
K. Wicksell: *Über Wert, Kapital und Rente*, 1893.
J. Schumpeter: *Das Rentenprin ip in der Verteilungslehre* (Schmollers Jahrbücher XXXI), 1907.
Wesen und Hauptinhalt der theoretischen Nationalökonomie, 1908.
Das Grundprinzip der Verteilungslehre (Arch. der Sozialwissenschaft, Bd. 42), 1917.

(b) BRITISH AND AMERICAN WRITERS

W. Smart: *Introduction to the Theory of Value*, 1891.
The Distribution of Income, 1899.
J. R. Commons: *The Distribution of Wealth*, 1893.

P. H. Wicksteed: *The Co-ordination of the Laws of Production and Distribution*, 1894.
    The Common Sense of Political Economy, 1910.
H. J. Davenport: *The Formula of Sacrifice* (J.P.E., II, p. 561), 1894.
    Proposed Modifications in the Austrian Theory (Q.J.E.), 1902.
    Value and Distribution, 1908.
    The Economics of Enterprise, 1913.
D. I. Greene: *Opportunity Cost* (Q.J.E., VIII, p. 218), 1894.
H. D. Henderson: *Supply and Demand*, 1922.

6. Modern Analytical School

A. and M. P. Marshall: *Economics of Industry*, 1881.
A. Marshall: *Principles of Economics*, 1890 (1920).
E. Cannan: *History of the Theories of Production and Distribution*, 1893.
    The Economic Outlook, 1912.
    Wealth, 1914.
    Review of Economic Theory, 1929.
V. Pareto: *Cours d'Economie Politique*, 1896.
J. B. Clark: *The Distribution of Wealth*, 1899 (1902).
    Essentials of Economic Theory, 1924.
F. W. Taussig: *Principles of Economics*, 1911 (1921).
A. C. Pigou: *Wealth and Welfare*, 1912.
    The Economics of Welfare, 1920 (1929).
    Essays in Applied Economics, 1923.
G. Cassel: *Theoretische Sozialökonomie*, 1918 (1931). (Trans. *The Theory of Social Economy*, 1923 (1931).)
    Fundamental Thoughts in Economics, 1925.
R. G. Hawtrey: *The Economic Problem*, 1926.

B. SPECIAL ASPECTS OF ECONOMIC THEORY

1. Theory of Wages

A. Menger: *Das Recht auf den vollen Arbeitsertrag*, 1886. (Trans. *The Right to the Whole Produce of Labour*, 1899.)
H. M. Thompson: *The Theory of Wages*, 1892.
T. N. Carver: *The Theory of Wages and Recent Theories of Value* (Q.J.E., VIII, p. 377), 1894.
F. W. Taussig: *Wages and Capital*, 1896.
B. and S. Webb: *Industrial Democracy*, 1902 (1920).
W. Beveridge: *Unemployment: a Problem of Industry*, 1909 (1930).
A. C. Pigou: *Unemployment*, 1913.
B. Webb: *The Wages of Men and Women: should they be Equal?* 1919.
D. H. Robertson: *Economic Incentive* (Economica), 1921.

F. Y. Edgworth: *Equal Pay to Men and Women for Equal Work* (E.J., XXXII), 1922.
F. Oppenheimer: *Der Arbeitslohn*, 1926.
L. Robbins: *Wages*, 1926.
N. Milnes: *The Economics of Wages and Labour*, 1926.
J. W. F. Rowe: *Wages in Practice and Theory*, 1928.
M. Dobb: *Wages*, 1928.

2. Theory of Interest

E. v. Böhm-Bawerk ⎫
K. Wicksell ⎬ See General Works on Economics.
T. N. Carver: *Abstinence and the Theory of Interest* (Q.J.E., VIII, p. 40), 1893.
G. Cassel: *The Nature and Necessity of Interest*, 1903.
I. Fisher: *The Nature of Capital and Income*, 1906.
    The Rate of Interest, 1907.
    The Theory of Interest, 1930.

3. Theory of Profit

V. Mataja: *Der Unternehmergewinn*, 1884.
F. Oppenheimer: *Wert und Kapitalprofit*, 1916.
F. H. Knight: *Risk, Uncertainty and Profit*, 1921.

4. Theory of Rent

D. Ricardo: *Principles of Political Economy and Taxation*, 1817.
E. Cannan: *History of Local Rates in England*, 1896 (1912).

5. Theory of International Trade

J. S. Mill: *Principles of Political Economy* (Bk. III, chap. xvii–xviii), 1848.
A. Marshall: *Pure Theory of Foreign Trade*, 1897 (1930).
C. F. Bastable: *Theory of International Trade*, 1903.
F. W. Taussig: *International Trade*, 1927.

INDEX